S0-AFB-467

THIS DIARY BELONGS TO

....

2019 Astrology Diary

Plan your year with the stars

Patsy Bennett

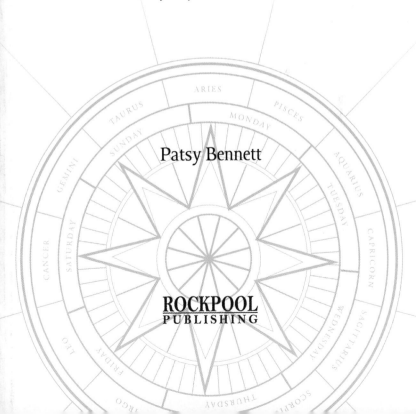

ROCKPOOL
PUBLISHING

A Rockpool book
PO Box 252
Summer Hill
NSW 2130
Australia
www.rockpoolpublishing.com.au
http://www.facebook.com/RockpoolPublishing

ISBN 978-1-925682-15-1
Northern Hemisphere edition

First published in 2019
Copyright Text © Patsy Bennett 2019
Copyright Design © Rockpool Publishing 2019
This edition published in 2019

Cover and internal design by Jessica Le, Rockpool Publishing
Typesetting by Marcella Cheng
Frontispiece by W. G. Evans, 1856, *Map of the Constellations in July, August, September*.
Other map illustrations by Alexander Jamieson, 1822, Celestial Atlas.
Glyph illustrations by http://All-Silhouettes.com, Zodiac illustrations by http://vectorian.net
Compass illustration by Jessica Le, Rockpool Publishing

Printed and bound in China

10 9 8 7 6 5 4 3 2 1

NB: The planetary phenomena and aspects listed on each day are set to Greenwich Mean Time (GMT) apart from the summer time (March 31st to October 27th) where they are set to British Summer Time. To convert times to your locations, please see www.timeanddate.com Astrological interpretations take into account all aspects and the sign the sun and planets are in on each day and are not taken out of context.

INTRODUCTION

Make 2019 your best year yet! This diary/planner is designed to help you make the most of your year. If you live your life by the Sun, Moon and Stars, you'll love the 2019 Astrology Diary: you'll have expert astrological advice right at your fingertips! I have interpreted major daily astrological data for you here in the diary pages, to help you plan ahead so that 2019 will be all you wish it to be.

Simply following the diary dates and the interpretations of astrological phenomena will help you plan ahead and enjoy your days. (Please see 'How to use this diary' for more details about terminology used in the diary pages).

The major themes for personal growth and success this year are:

- To develop and also to anchor the new adventures you began in 2018.
- To innovate, and expand your ideas and make them viable, practical and realistic.
- To look for healing, self-nurturing and self-empowerment through working with your true purpose and what brings you, personally, a sense of accomplishment.
- To understand authority and how nurturance – both of self and others – fits in the social fabric.

2019 really is the year where hard work will pay off, but it won't be all hard work and no play! There will be plenty of opportunities to enjoy life. When you love what you do every day, both at work and in your daily routine, life becomes so much more enjoyable. So why not plan now to incorporate at least one activity each day that makes your heart sing? This will have an exponential effect that produces a more fulfilling, enjoyable and resplendent year all-round.

The importance of self-nurture and health will be a recurring theme in 2019, because nothing can be done without good health, wellbeing, self-esteem and nurturance. This will become all the more apparent as the year unfolds.

Self-nurturance and nurturance of others can further your understanding of the workings of society and of authority figures and the parameters of authoritarian and cultural structures. Work to create structures in your own life that are healthy and provide balance and harmony, as these qualities will be key motivators this year.

The year begins with a partial solar eclipse on January 6th, followed by the total lunar eclipse on the 21st, which will create a heightened sense of change early in the year. And, if you believe change can feel destabilizing, look for ways to provide yourself with a solid platform so that you can be practical and take action in new and interesting, innovative ways during the year.

January really will set the pace for the year. You'll soon gain a lovely sense of progress – largely through the idea that change can be beneficial.

Uranus, the celestial game-changer, ends a lengthy (almost five-month) retrograde phase in January, thereby stimulating progress. The alignment of healer Chiron with Venus and the Moon's Nodes in January suggests that, where you feel you are on track already, you must keep going. Follow your dreams because your sense of purpose and self-empowerment will flower as a result.

Take advantage of Mars in Aries from January 1st until mid-February, as this will truly put the wind beneath your wings, especially for fire signs (Aries, Leo and Sagittarius) and cardinal signs (Aries, Cancer, Capricorn and Libra). Everyone has some fire in their astrological charts so take the cue from Mars, the planet astrologers associate with energy and vivacity, and find ways to feel revitalized. Then channel your energy into favorite pursuits, especially those that lead to a sense of accomplishment such as creative, musical, artistic and spiritual endeavors.

The influence of both Saturn and Pluto in Capricorn throughout the year will create a sense of stability, but also the motivation to work hard towards goals. A pitfall would be unwillingness to move ahead and becoming stuck in outworn habits and customs this year, so be wary of this. May through to mid-September are the months to watch the tendency to stick with bad and outworn habits; to be unwilling to move forward. But if you focus on regrouping, the period from May to mid-September will be excellent for planning to move forward once more with fresh ideas in the last quarter of the year.

Another pitfall this year would be day-dreaming, fatigue, lack of motivation and error that leads you astray. The decision is yours, as choices will arise throughout the year to work hard on manifesting your ideal scenario – or simply to give in at the first, second or third hurdles. And it's here that health (of mind, body and soul) will have such a strong influence this year; it's vital you shore up all your various energy levels so that you feel optimistic and are proactive.

Events in July may be the real test of your diligence and staying power, as there will be the temptation then to stay put, to stagnate rather than to steam ahead. And, while there is nothing 'wrong' with taking breaks and re-grouping, there is a very real risk that, for every three steps you take forward, you take four back at this time.

Luckily, there is a healing aspect to events in July that cannot be under-estimated, as Chiron, the celestial 'Wounded Healer', will align favourably with the Sun, Mercury and Mars in Leo, creating the ideal opportunity to move forward in therapeutic and uplifting, proactive ways.

However, the second eclipse season will fall in July, with a total solar eclipse on the 2nd, and then a partial lunar eclipse on the night of the 16th–17th. These eclipses will be across the Cancer–Capricorn axis, suggesting questions of authority, nurturing and home, and the best way to move forward work-wise and in your bigger-picture direction will come to a turning point. The topic of self-nurturance during times when you are under pressure, may peak; at this time the benefit of expert advice and the help of people with more wisdom and experience than you have, will be at a premium.

Once Jupiter ends a lengthy retrograde phase mid-August, aligning favorably with the Sun, Venus and Mars, there is every chance to boost the feel-good factor if you did fall in a rut mid-year.

Finally, with the Moon's North Node in Cancer for the entire year, and three of the four eclipses falling in Capricorn, this year is truly about how you will work in the big picture regarding self-nurturance; and how the ripple effect from this will improve both your entire life and the life of those you love.

Patsy x

How to use this diary

Solar, lunar and planetary movements

This diary lists the major solar, planetary and lunar movements day by day, and I have interpreted these so you can plan your days, weeks and months according to prevailing astrological trends. You'll gain insight into which days will be favorable for your planned events – from important meetings, get-togethers and celebrations to trips and life decisions; and which days will be variable, and which may even be frustrating. You'll see, when you plan your life by the stars, that sometimes, taking ill-timed action can lead to disappointment and that taking well-timed action will lead to success.

The Sun in the zodiac signs

Astrology is the study of the movement of celestial objects from our point of view here on Earth. We are most familiar with the study of our Sun signs, which depicts the movement and placement of the Sun in the zodiac signs Aries through to Pisces. In the same way the Sun moves through the zodiac signs Aries to Pisces through the calendar year, so do the planets and other celestial objects such as asteroid-planet Chiron.

This diary features monthly forecasts when the Sun is in each sign, beginning with the Sun in Capricorn (December 2018 to January 2019) and proceeding through the signs and finishing once again with the Sun in Capricorn in December 2019.

Each monthly forecast applies to everyone, as it is a general forecast for all Sun signs. There is also a forecast uniquely for your own particular Sun sign; so you'll find the 'For Capricorn' section is uniquely for Capricorns and so on. When the Sun is in your own sign, this can prove particularly motivational and is a great time to get ahead with projects that resonate with your self-esteem, gut instincts and bigger-picture motivation.

The Moon in the zodiac signs

Just as the Sun moves through the zodiac signs, so does the Moon. This diary lists these movements, as they can have a perceived influence over the mood and tone of the day, just as the Sun in different signs is known to characterize different traits. So where a diary entry states: 'The Moon enters Taurus', this indicates that the Moon has left the zodiac sign Aries, and has 'entered' the sign of Taurus, and will now reside in Taurus, until it moves on to Gemini in a couple of days' time.

New Moons and Full Moons are also listed in this diary, as these can mark turning points within your journey through the year. New Moons are generally a great time to begin a new project. Full Moons can signify a culmination or a peak in a project or event. So if you're planning to launch a business, or your children wish to begin a new course or activity, you can check in this diary if the day you're planning your event will be favorable for beginning a fresh venture. Simply check to see if your new venture falls on or near a New Moon, and also take a look at the diary entries either side of your proposed events, to ensure celestial influences will be working in your favor.

Eclipses can indicate particularly powerful turning points and it is for this reason eclipses are also listed in the diary dates. If a lunar- or solar eclipse is in the same sign as your own particular Sun sign, it may be particularly potent.

The phases of the Moon can truly influence the tone of your day, so this diary features every Moon sign, daily. The Moon remains in each sign approximately two days. Below, I've listed the mood depending on which sign the Moon is in, on a daily basis:

MOON IN ARIES: can bring an upbeat approach to life, but restlessness or fiery outbursts can result if you, or those around you, feel under pressure.

MOON IN TAURUS: can bring stability to feelings and routine, a sensual time and predilection for all things artistic and musical, but over-indulgence and stubbornness can result if under pressure.

MOON IN GEMINI: can bring a chatty, talkative approach to life, but flippancy, indecision and uncertainty can result if you, or those around you, feel under pressure.

MOON IN CANCER: a sense of security, nesting, cocooning and nurturance will be sought, for family time and those you love, but insecurities or a lack of adaptability can result if you feel under pressure.

MOON IN LEO: an upbeat approach to life and more dynamic attitude to others and yourself will arise, but a Leo Moon can bring arrogance, pride and vanity to the surface if under pressure.

MOON IN VIRGO: a great time to focus on health, routine, decluttering, work and being helpful, but over-analysis, obsessive attention to detail and ambivalence can also arise if under pressure.

MOON IN LIBRA: a lovely time to focus on art, music, love, creating harmony and peace, but a sense of disharmony, indecision and dissatisfaction can arise if you're under pressure.

Moon in Scorpio: a focus on personal needs, sensuality, enjoyment of life and indulgence in all things wonderful, but if under pressure, deep feelings emerge that are intense or potentially destructive.

Moon in Sagittarius: an outgoing, upbeat phase, when an adventurous attitude will bring out your joviality and lust for learning and life. When under pressure, you and others may appear blunt, or disregard others' feelings.

Moon in Capricorn: can stimulate a practical and focused approach to work, to your goals and plans. But when under pressure, a sense of limitations, restrictions and authoritarian strictures can arise.

Moon in Aquarius: a quirky, outgoing phase, when trying new activities and new approaches to life will appeal. When you're under pressure, Moon in Aquarius may stimulate unreliability, unconventionality or changeability.

Moon in Pisces: a dreamy, introverted or artistic time in which music, the arts and romance will thrive. A good time for meditation. When you're under pressure, a Pisces Moon can bring excessive daydreaming, forgetfulness, vagueness.

NB: If you know your Moon sign, you may find that when the Moon is in your sign, as listed in this diary, life is easier – or more challenging – depending on the planetary aspects to your Moon at the time of your birth. Keep a note of the general mood or occurrences when the Moon is in your sign and you may find that a pattern emerges.

Interplanetary aspects

Astrologers also study the movements of planets in relation to each other. The measurements are in degrees, minutes and seconds. These measurements focus on patterns and particular aspects, which are the angles between the planets, the Sun and other celestial objects. This diary includes mention of these aspects between the Sun and the planets, and the terminology used is explained below – from 'opposition' (when a planet is opposite another) to 'quincunx' (when a planet is at a 150-degree angle to another).

The angles the planets and the Sun make to one another have meanings in astrology. For example, a 'trine' aspect (120-degree angle) can be considered beneficial for the progress of your plans; a 'square' aspect (90-degree angle) can present as a challenge (depending on your own attitude to challenges and obstacles).

By choosing dates carefully for the fruition of your plans, you will be moving forward with the benefit of the knowledge of the cosmic influences that can help your progress. NB: When you read the planetary aspects in this diary, such as 'Sun square Uranus', be aware that the aspect's influence may span to a day before and a day after the actual date it is entered in this diary, especially regarding outer planets (Neptune, Uranus and Pluto). However, the Moon phases are relevant for each day.

Planetary aspects:

CONJUNCTION: when a celestial object is at the same degree and generally in the same sign of the zodiac as another celestial object and therefore is aligned from our point of view here on Earth. This can intensify the dynamics between the celestial objects and Earth.

OPPOSITION: when a planet is opposite another, at a 180-degree angle. This can intensify the inter-planetary dynamics.

SEXTILE: A 60-degree angle. This can be a peaceful, harmonious influence, or facilitate the flow of energy between planetary influences.

SEMI-SEXTILE: A 30-degree angle. This is a harmonious aspect or facilitates the flow of energy between planetary influences.

SQUARE: A 90-degree angle. This can be a challenging aspect, but as some people 'get going when the going gets tough', it can lead to a breakthrough.

TRINE: A 120-degree angle. This can be a peaceful, harmonious influence, or facilitate the flow of energy between planetary influences.

QUINCUNX: A 150-degree angle. This can present a hurdle to be overcome.

Retrogrades

Planets can appear to go backwards, from our point of view here on Earth. The best known retrograde phases are those of Mercury and Venus, although all other planets also turn retrograde, and these retrograde phases are mentioned in this diary, too. Retrograde phases can be a good time to assimilate, consolidate and integrate recent developments, although traditionally, retrograde phases are associated with delays, a slow-down or difficult process. For example, a Mercury retrograde phase is often associated with difficult communications or traffic snarls, and yet it can be an excellent time to integrate events, and to consolidate, review and re-order your ideas. This diary lists start – and finish – dates of Mercury retrograde phases, as well as the kinds of activities that may be influenced by this phenomenon and in the same sign of the zodiac.

A 'station' is when planets 'turn' from one direction to the other, from our point of view here on Earth.

2019 NORTHERN HEMISPHERE MOON PHASES

JANUARY

S	M	T	W	T	F	S
		1	2	3	4	5
		☾	☾	☾	☾	☾
6	7	8	9	10	11	12
○	☽	☽	☽	☽	☽	☽
13	14	15	16	17	18	19
☽	☽	●	●	●	●	●
20	21	22	23	24	25	26
●	●	●	●	●	●	☾
27	28	29	30	31		
☾	☾	☾	☾	☾		

FEBRUARY

S	M	T	W	T	F	S
					1	2
					☾	☾
3	4	5	6	7	8	9
☾	○	☽	☽	☽	☽	☽
10	11	12	13	14	15	16
☽	☽	●	●	●	●	●
17	18	19	20	21	22	23
●	●	●	●	●	●	☾
24	25	26	27	28		
☾	☾	☾	☾	☾		

MARCH

S	M	T	W	T	F	S
31					1	2
☾					☾	☾
3	4	5	6	7	8	9
☾	☾	☾	○	☽	☽	☽
10	11	12	13	14	15	16
☽	☽	☽	☽	●	●	●
17	18	19	20	21	22	23
●	●	●	●	●	●	●
24	25	26	27	28	29	30
●	●	●	☾	☾	☾	☾

APRIL

S	M	T	W	T	F	S
	1	2	3	4	5	6
	☾	☾	☾	☾	○	☽
7	8	9	10	11	12	13
☽	☽	☽	☽	☽	☽	●
14	15	16	17	18	19	20
●	●	●	●	●	●	●
21	22	23	24	25	26	27
●	●	●	●	☾	☾	☾
28	29	30				
☾	☾	☾				

MAY

S	M	T	W	T	F	S
			1	2	3	4
			☾	☾	☾	○
5	6	7	8	9	10	11
☽	☽	☽	☽	☽	☽	●
12	13	14	15	16	17	18
●	●	●	●	●	●	●
19	20	21	22	23	24	25
●	●	●	●	☾	☾	☾
26	27	28	29	30	31	
☾	☾	☾	☾	☾	☾	

JUNE

S	M	T	W	T	F	S
30						1
☾						☾
2	3	4	5	6	7	8
☾	○	☽	☽	☽	☽	☽
9	10	11	12	13	14	15
☽	☽	●	●	●	●	●
16	17	18	19	20	21	22
●	●	●	●	●	●	●
23	24	25	26	27	28	29
☾	☾	☾	☾	☾	☾	☾

2019 NORTHERN HEMISPHERE MOON PHASES

JULY

S	M	T	W	T	F	S
	1	2	3	4	5	6
7	8	9	10	11	12	13
14	15	16	17	18	19	20
21	22	23	24	25	26	27
28	29	30	31			

AUGUST

S	M	T	W	T	F	S
				1	2	3
4	5	6	7	8	9	10
11	12	13	14	15	16	17
18	19	20	21	22	23	24
25	26	27	28	29	30	31

SEPTEMBER

S	M	T	W	T	F	S
1	2	3	4	5	6	7
8	9	10	11	12	13	14
15	16	17	18	19	20	21
22	23	24	25	26	27	28
29	30					

OCTOBER

S	M	T	W	T	F	S
		1	2	3	4	5
6	7	8	9	10	11	12
13	14	15	16	17	18	19
20	21	22	23	24	25	26
27	28	29	30	31		

NOVEMBER

S	M	T	W	T	F	S
					1	2
3	4	5	6	7	8	9
10	11	12	13	14	15	16
17	18	19	20	21	22	23
24	25	26	27	28	29	30

DECEMBER

S	M	T	W	T	F	S
1	2	3	4	5	6	7
8	9	10	11	12	13	14
15	16	17	18	19	20	21
22	23	24	25	26	27	28
29	30	31				

○ New Moon ● Full Moon

JANUARY 2019

The Sun entered Capricorn, December 21st, 2018

The Sun in the earthy sign of Capricorn always highlights the merits of hard work and diligence and, at this time of year, we get to congratulate ourselves after all the hard work of the year as we take a break at Christmas.

The big news in January will be the eclipses and these will spotlight status, personal contribution to community and free will. In other words, how do you feel you are progressing in your life in the bigger picture: do you feel valued; are you able to express your core values in your community and at work; and what are your long-term plans to feel more fulfilled, both at work and at home?

Early January will be an excellent time to strategize once Uranus ends its lengthy, five-month retrograde phase on January 6th, and you may even experience an out-of-the-ordinary revelation or event that truly adds direction so early in the year.

The Sun and three planets in staid and traditional Capricorn may however, contribute to the sense that there is value in keeping with the tried and the trusted. You will get the chance to decide the relative merits of moving forward versus keeping things as they are, but the eclipses will at the very least offer alternatives to your existing circumstances.

Your task will be to evaluate where your priorities lie. Intense or changeable circumstances around January 11th should concede to more certainty about the best way forward mid-month, so trust your instincts and look for ways to progress in the most practical way possible.

The Neptune-Jupiter 'Square' in January may predispose you to daydreaming and idealism, so maintain your foothold in reality while reaching for the stars.

For Capricorns:

This is an excellent month to instigate new strategies and timetables, but you must keep new ventures manageable and realistic. This is largely because events in January will stimulate your imagination, inspiration and innovation, and may also signal a change in your romantic, artistic or creative endeavors.

The Capricorn solar eclipse on the 6th very much suggests you consider a new approach to life, one that involves more magic and synchronicity, more creativity and art. However, you may also be liable to be easily influenced at this time, so ensure you cross-check your new and inspired ideas with facts and figures. Otherwise, you may feel uncomfortable following inspiration rather than cold, hard facts, causing you to feel disorientated rather than liberated.

For some Capricorns, January will represent the opportunity to reconnect with yourself, and this may bring into question some of your relationships. The lunar eclipse on January 21st will spotlight your relationships with partners, both business and personal, and should reinvigorate relationships, especially if you took the chance earlier in the month to figure out exactly where you wish to be heading in 2019, especially in your personal life.

INTENTIONS *for the* YEAR

Venus in virgo

Mars in cancer

MONDAY 31 ☾

TUESDAY 1 ☾

Moon in Scorpio.

WEDNESDAY 2 ☾

Sun conjunct Saturn; Sun semi-sextile Jupiter: decisions can be made, and if you feel the weight of responsibility now, ensure you're happy with decisions you make. A light-hearted attitude could direct you to a fun event.
Moon enters Sagittarius.

THURSDAY 3 ☾

Moon in Sagittarius.

FRIDAY 4

32° N 30' 117° WO

Mercury trine Uranus: unexpected news or visitors may arrive. You may have a light-bulb moment. Moon enters Capricorn.

mars in cancer
passive- aggresiveness
resist change
direct confrontation

SATURDAY 5

Moon in Capricorn.

secure b4 act
"the best offense is defense"
tenacious

SUNDAY 6

Partial solar eclipse in Capricorn; Uranus ends its retrograde phase: an interesting turn of events will illuminate your options. This will be a good time to make plans and to strategize.

		JANUARY				
S	M	T	W	T	F	S
		1	2	3	4	5
6	7	8	9	10	11	12
13	14	15	16	17	18	19
20	21	22	23	24	25	26
27	28	29	30	31		

MONDAY 7)

Moon enters Aquarius.

TUESDAY 8)

Mercury square Mars: you may feel at cross-purposes with someone today.
Avoid misunderstandings. Projects can excel if you're careful with details.
Moon in Aquarius.

WEDNESDAY 9)

Moon enters Pisces.

THURSDAY 10)

Moon in Pisces.

FRIDAY 11 ☽

Sun conjunct Pluto: you may have intense feelings today. Ensure you have the right facts. Moon in Pisces.

SATURDAY 12 ☽

Moon enters Aries.

SUNDAY 13 ☽

Mercury conjunct Saturn; Jupiter square Neptune: news arrives. A good day for meetings and communications at work, but you must check details and avoid allowing your imagination to run away with you. Moon in Aries.

		JANUARY				
S	M	T	W	T	F	S
		1	2	3	4	5
6	7	8	9	10	11	12
13	14	15	16	17	18	19
20	21	22	23	24	25	26
27	28	29	30	31		

MONDAY 14 ☽

Mercury sextile Neptune; Mercury semi-sextile Jupiter: you'll enjoy giving your imagination free rein; talks could be uplifting. Art and romance will appeal. Moon enters Taurus.

TUESDAY 15 ☽

Moon in Taurus.

WEDNESDAY 16 ☽

Moon in Taurus.

THURSDAY 17 ☽

Moon enters Gemini.

FRIDAY 18 ●

Venus trine Mars; Mercury conjunct Pluto; Sun square Uranus; Sun sextile Chiron: a day of contrasts and high energy. If entering contracts, ensure you have all the details. Someone may be changeable. Moon in Gemini.

SATURDAY 19 ●

Moon enters Cancer.

SUNDAY 20 ●

The Sun enters Aquarius: think outside the square and prepare to be adaptable. Venus semi-sextile Saturn: agreements can be made, as long as you have the facts. Moon in Cancer.

			JANUARY			
S	M	T	W	T	F	S
		1	2	3	4	5
6	7	8	9	10	11	12
13	14	15	16	17	18	19
20	21	22	23	24	25	26
27	28	29	30	31		

January to February 2019

Sun enters Aquarius, January 20th

A dominant theme will revolve around how well you adapt to change. As Venus aligns with Jupiter, and both planets aspect pioneering Mars harmoniously, you may be inclined to step into new territory or to begin a fresh venture. The key to being able to adapt to change will lie in having the details you need at your fingertips, so ensure you underpin your new-found circumstances with research and realistic expectations. Your goals will be more attainable when you work towards them methodically.

The total lunar eclipse and Supermoon on January 21st will open new doors for you, principally breathing new life into your routine. This may involve a new look at yourself and what you stand for, or literally a new look!

The Aquarian New Moon on February 4th will encourage you to resurrect ideas that may have seemed a little left-field or even unattainable in the past, and to make changes to action revitalizing and inspired ideas.

Once Mars aligns with Uranus on February 13th, your ideas should be actionable. However, if you feel a little restless at this time too, avoid making changes merely out of restlessness. The key to success really does lie in good research and fundamental facts.

With St Valentine's Day falling so close to the Mars–Uranus alignment, avoid rash moves but be open, nevertheless, for love to strike where it may!

Mercury and Neptune in Pisces could be inspirational in the second half of February – but you may also tend to daydream or to be easily misled. The last two weeks of February are particularly ideal for the arts and writing, so plan then to create some beautiful work.

For Aquarians:

The total lunar eclipse and Supermoon in Leo on January 21st will truly set you thinking about your personal life. It's time for a fresh approach. You may even wonder whether there is a fated, pre-destined quality to events this month, and how you will work with these in your personal life. If you find that a partnership, business or personal, is at a turning point, evaluate how you wish to progress, especially as you may find that you are tending to re-evaluate your ideas and values.

For many Aquarians, the lunar eclipse will mark a fresh daily routine, a fresh phase at work or simply the chance to turn a leaf health-wise and in your work-life balance.

If you feel inclined to avoid rocking the boat, personal motivation and ambition may egg you on to make changes. The Aquarian New Moon on February 4th will further add incentive to turn a new leaf, especially in your personal life. However, you may wish to err on the side of caution as you value the stability and security some aspects of your life provide.

Information will be the catalyst to taking the right course of action. And, once Mercury joins Neptune in Pisces from the 11th, your inspiration really will guide you so much better than it did earlier in the year, and you should feel more sure-footed about the decisions you make.

MONDAY 21 ●

Total lunar eclipse and Supermoon in Leo; Venus square Neptune; Mars square Saturn: be ready to view yourself and your values in a new light. This may involve the way you see yourself in relation to others. Avoid hasty decisions.

TUESDAY 22 ●

Venus conjunct Jupiter: a romantic day; you could make great headway with a special project. Moon in Leo.

WEDNESDAY 23 ●

Mercury square Uranus; Mercury sextile Chiron: expect unexpected news or developments. Avoid misunderstandings. Tense topics may be discussed with a view to agreement or healing. Moon enters Virgo.

THURSDAY 24 ●

Mercury enters Aquarius: communications will become more inspired, but some talks could seem stuck. If so, it's time for a fresh approach. Moon in Virgo.

FRIDAY 25

Mars trine Jupiter: an adventurous idea could work. Moon enters Libra.

SATURDAY 26

Moon in Libra.

SUNDAY 27

Venus semi-sextile Pluto: love and romance may be on your mind; agreements can be made. Moon enters Scorpio.

| | | JANUARY | | | | |
S	M	T	W	T	F	S
		1	2	3	4	5
6	7	8	9	10	11	12
13	14	15	16	17	18	19
20	21	22	23	24	25	26
27	28	29	30	31		

MONDAY 28 ◖

Moon in Scorpio.

TUESDAY 29 ◖

Sun conjunct Mercury: a good day to talk. A trip or visit may be relevant. Moon enters Sagittarius.

WEDNESDAY 30 ◖

Moon in Sagittarius.

THURSDAY 31 ◖

Saturn sextile Neptune: you'll feel inspired to put ideal plans in motion. Moon in Sagitarius.

FRIDAY 1 ⟨

Moon enters Capricorn.

SATURDAY 2 ⟨

*Venus trine Uranus; Mars square Pluto: check details and avoid impulsiveness
and misunderstandings. Have you romanticized an event? Avoid misplacing
belongings. A surprising event may arise. Moon in Capricorn.*

SUNDAY 3 ⟨

*Venus enters Capricorn: you may feel increasingly that stability and security
are important to you. Mercury sextile Jupiter: good news or a trip may be in
the cards. Venus square Chiron: avoid taking random comments personally.
Moon enters Aquarius.*

FEBRUARY

S	M	T	W	T	F	S
					1	2
3	4	5	6	7	8	9
10	11	12	13	14	15	16
17	18	19	20	21	22	23
24	25	26	27	28		

MONDAY 4 ○

Aquarius New Moon: new ideas and plans will feel invigorating.
Time for change.

TUESDAY 5 ☽

Mercury semi-sextile Pluto: communications could open new options.
Moon in Aquarius.

WEDNESDAY 6 ☽

Moon enters Pisces.

THURSDAY 7 ☽

Moon in Pisces.

FRIDAY 8 ❯

Sun sextile Jupiter and Mercury sextile Mars: you may be attracted to out-of-the-ordinary ventures over the next nine weeks, or feel like breaking into new territory. Good for communications and research; information comes to light. Avoid impulsiveness, but keep an eye out for news. Moon enters Aries.

SATURDAY 9 ❯

Mercury sextile Uranus: expect an unusual or out-of-the-ordinary event or news. A good day for meetings. Moon in Aries.

SUNDAY 10 ❯

Mercury enters Pisces; Sun semi-sextile Pluto: you'll feel inspired to follow a dream over coming weeks. Romance, art, music and film will all feel inspiring. Moon in Aries.

FEBRUARY

S	M	T	W	T	F	S
					1	2
3	4	5	6	7	8	9
10	11	12	13	14	15	16
17	18	19	20	21	22	23
24	25	26	27	28		

MONDAY 11

Moon enters Taurus.

TUESDAY 12

Moon in Taurus.

WEDNESDAY 13

Mars conjunct Uranus. You may be inclined to act rashly, or experience an unusual or out-of-the-blue event. Stick with facts. Moon enters Gemini.

THURSDAY 14

Mars enters Taurus: you will feel inclined to follow your heart over the coming six weeks, perhaps more than usual. Moon in Gemini.

FRIDAY 15 ●

Moon enters Cancer.

SATURDAY 16 ●

Moon in Cancer.

SUNDAY 17 ●

Venus sextile Neptune: romance will appeal, as will art, reading, music and film. Moon enters Leo.

			FEBRUARY			
S	M	T	W	T	F	S
					1	2
3	4	5	6	7	8	9
10	11	12	13	14	15	16
17	18	19	20	21	22	23
24	25	26	27	28		

FEBRUARY TO MARCH 2019

Sun enters Pisces, February 18th

The Sun in Pisces is associated with a dreamy, philosophical, inspired time and, this year, the theme of nurturance and healing will be just as prevalent. The planet-asteroid Chiron enters Aries at the same time as the Sun enters Pisces, stimulating motivation to heal areas of your life that are stagnant – and literally to heal yourself if you are fatigued. This applies especially to Aries, Leo and Sagittarius, although all Sun signs may benefit from more self-nurturance at this time. If you are a teacher or you work in the medical arena, you may be particularly busy.

The Virgo Full Moon and Supermoon on February 19th will spotlight where a change in your daily routine could apply, so your activities fit better with your beliefs, and responsibilities. Health practices and the chance for more work-life balance may become a part of the equation.

Keep an eye on information and its reliability. Towards the end of February, you may discover information that is incorrect, or discover details that you must research.

You may even be surprised early March to learn new information that puts you on a fresh course of action. Try to get important paperwork signed and completed before Mercury turns retrograde on March 5th (Mercury will be retrograde until March 28th). This phase will be excellent to review your accomplishments this year, and to stabilise various initiatives so that you are happy to progress once life speeds ahead in April. The Pisces New Moon on March 6th should prove inspiring, especially as developments you have worked on in previous years should begin to show results. The entry of Uranus into Taurus on the same day represents a major turning point, especially for Aquarians, Pisceans, Virgos, Taureans, Scorpios and Leos, although everyone is likely to feel inspired to broaden their horizons in new areas over coming months — some you may not have even considered before.

Key news or developments mid-March could be significant; follow your instincts and be adventurous.

For Pisces:

This is a wonderful month to turn a page in your personal life, and financially. The Virgo Full Moon and Supermoon on February 19th will spotlight a relationship, business or personal, and particularly your approach to someone's habits, health and wellbeing. Perhaps you can do more for them? Perhaps you have already done too much, and are exhausted? This Full Moon will encourage you to alter circumstances so that you gain a healthier attitude and more vibrant daily routine.

The Pisces New Moon on March 6th will further encourage you to turn a corner. To do this, you may ask: where do I derive a sense of stability? Who and what provides me with a sense of purpose and belonging? You may be surprised by who steps forward to offer support.

You may also be surprised by the draw towards freedom, especially where this relates to overseas, learning, sports, and perhaps even legal matters. Your task will be to weigh up how important being inspired and freedom of movement is, versus stabilise and security.

MONDAY 18 ●

Sun enters Pisces; Chiron enters Aries; Sun sextile Uranus; Venus conjunct Saturn: it's all change! You may need to commit to a new idea or venture. Be bold but check the facts. Moon in Leo.

TUESDAY 19 ●

Full Moon Supermoon in Virgo; Mercury conjunct Neptune: ideal for a detox, cleanse, get-together and for paperwork. Avoid misunderstandings and absent-mindedness.

WEDNESDAY 20 ●

Moon in Virgo.

THURSDAY 21 ●

Venus semi-sextile Jupiter: a lovely day for romance, art and meetings with people you love. Moon enters Libra.

FRIDAY 22 ●

Mercury square Jupiter: you can get ahead with important talks today, but you must be careful to avoid exaggeration and idealism. Moon in Libra.

SATURDAY 23 ●

Mercury sextile Pluto; Venus conjunct Pluto: conversations or a trip may be intense, but could lead somewhere new. Moon enters Scorpio.

SUNDAY 24 ●

Moon in Scorpio.

		FEBRUARY				
S	M	T	W	T	F	S
					1	2
3	4	5	6	7	8	9
10	11	12	13	14	15	16
17	18	19	20	21	22	23
24	25	26	27	28		

MONDAY 25

Moon enters Sagittarius.

TUESDAY 26

Moon in Sagittarius.

WEDNESDAY 27

Sun sextile Mars: you can get ahead with your projects and ideas today; just avoid impulsiveness. Moon in Sagittarius.

THURSDAY 28

Moon enters Capricorn.

FRIDAY 1   (

Venus enters Aquarius; Venus square Uranus: expect an unexpected event or a change of plan. Moon in Capricorn.

SATURDAY 2   (

Moon enters Aquarius.

SUNDAY 3   (

Moon in Aquarius.

		MARCH				
S	M	T	W	T	F	S
					1	2
3	4	5	6	7	8	9
10	11	12	13	14	15	16
17	18	19	20	21	22	23
24	25	26	27	28	29	30
31						

MONDAY 4   (

Moon in Aquarius.

TUESDAY 5   (

Mercury turns retrograde: the next three weeks will be ideal for revising and reviewing communications and developments so far this year. You may be drawn to reconnect with the past via communications or travel, for example. Moon enters Pisces.

WEDNESDAY 6   ○

New Moon in Pisces and Uranus enters Taurus: your philosophical, artistic, dreamy and spiritual side is likely to emerge over coming weeks. Romance will appeal. You may surprise yourself today.

THURSDAY 7   )

Sun conjunct Neptune; Jupiter semi-sextile Pluto: You may feel inspired by art and music or by someone romantic. Change could be for the better; you can make changes today. Moon enters Aries.

PISCES

FRIDAY 8)

Moon in Aries.

SATURDAY 9)

Sun sextile Saturn. A good day to be practical, grounded. A fatherly figure may be supportive. Seek expert advice if needed. Moon in Aries.

SUNDAY 10)

Mars sextile Neptune: you'll enjoy taking your plans to the next level. Moon enters Taurus.

			MARCH			
S	M	T	W	T	F	S
					1	2
3	4	5	6	7	8	9
10	11	12	13	14	15	16
17	18	19	20	21	22	23
24	25	26	27	28	29	30
31						

MONDAY 11 ❯

Moon in Taurus.

TUESDAY 12 ❯

Moon enters Gemini.

WEDNESDAY 13 ❯

Moon in Gemini.

THURSDAY 14 ▶

Sun square Jupiter; Mars trine Saturn: you could make great headway today at work but you must avoid being impulsive, especially if your views or wishes clash with someone else's. Optimism may pay off but you must set your sights realistically and be prepared to be adaptable. Moon enters Cancer.

FRIDAY 15 ◗

Sun conjunct Mercury; Mercury square Jupiter; Venus semi-square Neptune: art and romance will appeal and key news could arrive. Chores may need to be completed before you can relax. Avoid mix-ups today. Moon in Cancer.

SATURDAY 16 ◗

Mercury sextile Pluto: choose words carefully, and you could attain a goal or make key changes. Moon in Cancer.

SUNDAY 17 ◗

Moon enters Leo.

		MARCH				
S	M	T	W	T	F	S
					1	2
3	4	5	6	7	8	9
10	11	12	13	14	15	16
17	18	19	20	21	22	23
24	25	26	27	28	29	30
31						

MARCH TO
APRIL 2019

Sun enters Aries, March 20th

When the Sun enters Aries, this marks the spring equinox in the northern hemisphere. It's a time when we see new shoots of growth in the landscape and, likewise, we can look for ways to boost our projects so that they may blossom. The Sun's alignment with Chiron on March 22nd will signal you're ready to take action regarding personal growth where, in the past, you have been inclined to let things unfold as they may.

The Aries New Moon on April 5th will further add to the proactive mood, especially in those areas of your life where you've been careful to put clever ideas in place. Mars in Taurus until the end of March will help you build a strong framework that will grow your ideas. Be guided by ventures and people who truly appeal to you. Have faith that opportunities are indeed options that could build a better future.

Venus in Pisces in April will heighten your senses and appreciation for art, romance, music and dance. April is the ideal month to combine ideals with practicalities to forge ahead with exciting plans and projects. Mars in chatty Gemini will further add to the proactive tone in April: get set to succeed and don't be afraid to communicate your great ideas! Avoid being led by expectations alone from April 10th to 15th. If logistics prove complex, take a step back and consider your plan step by step.

The Full Moon in Libra on April 19th will provide the ideal scenario to regain a sense of balance if the actions you have taken have stretched your capabilities or ask that you enter new territory. Maintain positive affirmations mid-April as you set sail to a new understanding of someone close – and yourself, and especially what you're capable of. You can do it!

For Aries:

The big news is that Uranus, the planet that has ushered in so much change and restlessness over the past few years, has left your sign for the next 76 years, giving you the opportunity to consolidate recent developments and find more stability in life. You may be ready for a fresh set of values, largely as the result of the radical changes that have occurred over the years. The Full Moon and Supermoon in Libra, on March 21st, and the Chiron-Sun alignment on March 22nd, may point out a vulnerability that you would like to overcome. The end of March is, for this reason, a fairly healing time, ideal for setting aside time to strengthen yourself and to establish balance in life.

The Aries New Moon on April 5th will motivate you to see the world through new eyes. The important motivator here will be whether you feel fulfilled, or whether you are walking someone else's path. Singles born around this date should mingle, as you may meet someone caring and attentive. Couples will appreciate the chance to call peace if arguments have been rife. Luckily, Mercury will be in Aries from April 17th until May 7th, boosting your communication skills and kudos.

The second Libran Full Moon (on April 19th) will create the ideal scenario to establish harmony and peace in your life as a whole, even if this arises in out-of-the-ordinary ways. Ensure you don't miss the opportunity.

MONDAY 18 ●

Mercury semi-sextile Venus; Mercury sextile Mars: good for communications, a short trip and research; information comes to light. Avoid impulsiveness, but keep an eye out for news. Moon in Leo.

TUESDAY 19 ●

Moon enters Virgo.

WEDNESDAY 20 ●

Sun enters Aries: spring equinox; Mars trine Pluto; Mercury sextile Saturn: a good day to consider new plans and to put ideas into action. Moon in Virgo.

THURSDAY 21 ●

Full Moon and Supermoon in Libra; Venus square Mars; Venus sextile Jupiter: expect unexpected news or developments. Avoid impulsiveness. You could excel today with hard work and concentration and with the aim of finding balance.

FRIDAY 22 ●

Sun conjunct Chiron: this is a healing day, ideal for a healthy treat. You or someone close may feel vulnerable or sensitive, so take things step by step. Moon in Libra.

SATURDAY 23 ●

Moon enters Scorpio.

SUNDAY 24 ●

Mercury conjunct Neptune: you may feel idealistic, dreamy and philosophical. Keep an eye on facts and avoid forgetfulness. Moon in Scorpio.

			MARCH			
S	M	T	W	T	F	S
					1	2
3	4	5	6	7	8	9
10	11	12	13	14	15	16
17	18	19	20	21	22	23
24	25	26	27	28	29	30
31						

MONDAY 25

Moon enters Sagittarius.

TUESDAY 26

Venus enters Pisces: thoughts of lofty ideals, such as art, philosophy and generally finding value and meaning in life, will occupy the mind in coming weeks. You may consider beauty in a new light. Moon in Sagittarius.

WEDNESDAY 27

Venus sextile Uranus: an event may surprise you today. A good day to consider new options and projects. Moon enters Capricorn.

THURSDAY 28

Mercury ends its retrograde phase; you'll feel ready to get ahead with communications and travel ideas. Moon in Capricorn.

FRIDAY 29 ☾

Moon in Capricorn.

SATURDAY 30 ☾

Moon enters Aquarius.

SUNDAY 31 ☾

Mars enters Gemini: communications are likely to be busy for the next six weeks. Travel and new activities may appeal. Avoid impulsive decisions. Moon in Aquarius.

			MARCH			
S	M	T	W	T	F	S
					1	2
3	4	5	6	7	8	9
10	11	12	13	14	15	16
17	18	19	20	21	22	23
24	25	26	27	28	29	30
31						

MONDAY 1   (

Moon enters Pisces.

TUESDAY 2   (

Mercury conjunct Neptune: you may feel idealistic, dreamy, philosophical, romantic. Avoid absent-mindedness. Moon in Pisces.

WEDNESDAY 3   (

Moon in Pisces.

THURSDAY 4   (

Moon enters Aries.

FRIDAY 5 ○

New Moon in Aries: a great time to begin new projects and to be bolder or more independent if this appeals to you.

SATURDAY 6 ☽

Moon enters Taurus.

SUNDAY 7 ☽

Mercury sextile Saturn: a good day to make solid plans and to take practical action with travel, communications and work. Moon in Taurus.

		APRIL				
S	M	T	W	T	F	S
	1	2	3	4	5	6
7	8	9	10	11	12	13
14	15	16	17	18	19	20
21	22	23	24	25	26	27
28	29	30				

MONDAY 8)

Moon enters Gemini.

TUESDAY 9)

Moon in Gemini.

WEDNESDAY 10)

Venus conjunct Neptune; Sun square Saturn; Jupiter turns retrograde: the arts, love, film and music will appeal. A good time for romance. Avoid idealism. Check that you're not looking at the world through rose-coloured glasses or being stubborn. Consider parameters as guidelines rather than restrictions. An authority figure may be consulted.
Moon in Gemini.

THURSDAY 11)

Moon enters Cancer.

FRIDAY 12 ❯

Mercury square Jupiter; Sun square Moon's Nodes; Venus sextile Saturn: avoid misunderstandings and conflict; look for practical solutions and plan travel ahead to avoid delays. Moon in Cancer.

SATURDAY 13 ❯

Sun square Pluto: you may feel challenged by someone else's might and power. Rise to the challenge by being practical and adventurous. Avoid power struggles. Moon enters Leo.

SUNDAY 14 ❯

Sun trine Jupiter; Venus sextile Pluto: a lucky break or upbeat news is on the way. A good day to make changes you've researched. Moon in Leo.

APRIL

S	M	T	W	T	F	S
	1	2	3	4	5	6
7	8	9	10	11	12	13
14	15	16	17	18	19	20
21	22	23	24	25	26	27
28	29	30				

MONDAY 15

Venus square Jupiter: you can achieve a great deal today. Avoid conflict of opinions and exaggeration. Strong desires may need to be tempered. Check your values and priorities. Moon enters Virgo.

TUESDAY 16

Moon in Virgo.

WEDNESDAY 17

Mercury enters Aries: communications may be busy, or more upbeat. You and those around you may feel feisty or bolder than usual over the next two weeks. Moon enters Libra.

THURSDAY 18

Moon in Libra.

FRIDAY 19 ●

Full Moon in Libra: relationships and maintaining peace and harmony will be a focus. Moon enters Scorpio in the afternoon.

SATURDAY 20 ●

Sun enters Taurus; Venus enters Aries; Mercury conjunct Chiron: you may hear news to do with health and wellbeing or wish to boost fitness. Avoid taking random comments personally. This will be an earthy, sensual and practical four weeks. Moon in Scorpio.

SUNDAY 21 ●

Sun semi-sextile Venus: you'll enjoy a treat. Moon enters Sagittarius.

			APRIL			
S	M	T	W	T	F	S
	1	2	3	4	5	6
7	8	9	10	11	12	13
14	15	16	17	18	19	20
21	22	23	24	25	26	27
28	29	30				

APRIL TO MAY 2019

Sun enters Taurus, April 20th

Just as the Sun steps into Taurus on April 20th, Mercury, Venus and Chiron will gain ground in Aries, bringing key topics and communications center-stage – in no uncertain terms. With all this action in Aries, despite the Sun in Taurus at this time, there are likely to be feisty interactions or even temper tantrums at the end of April. So spare a thought that some people may be feeling sensitive, and practise patience for the sake of everyone's peace of mind.

Venus in its own sign of Taurus from mid-May onwards will provide respite from an otherwise edgy four weeks, so make plans to use this feisty and dynamic energy to get things done rather than be distracted by controversy or even conflict. Channel intense or high energy into activities that you enjoy and that can further your sense of fulfilment. Indulge the senses and boost wellbeing in practical ways.

From now until early October there will be between four and five planets retrograde, depending on the month, contributing potentially to a sense of being stuck, or of events simply not moving forward as well as you'd like them to.

To avoid feeling stuck, take advantage of the New Moon energy on May 4th, which can help you to boost self-esteem and self-worth, helping you to forge ahead courageously. The New Moon phase will also be an excellent time to consider how you mean to be practical in all areas of your life, not least financially; in other words, how can your inspired projects work long term, in realistic terms?

Avoid impulsive moves early in the month of May and work with teachers and those with more experience than you to move forward in life. The transformative Scorpio Full Moon on May 18th will coincide with a Mercury-Saturn trine that will be super helpful for communications and getting plans in gear. Mark this day, and those shortly before, as excellent days to make the changes you wish to see in your life in practical terms.

For Taureans:

Uranus, the planet that brings revolutionary change, will be in Taurus for the next six years, bringing key developments your way. Not only will you have the Sun in your sign during the next four weeks, which will feel revitalizing, but you will also enjoy Uranus in your sign bringing focus to changes you have instigated or considered already in 2017–18. You now have the chance to build on exciting plans.

The feisty mood this month could add to a spiky, uncomfortable feel for you, as you like to take things step by step. With your sign's ruler, Venus, in upbeat Aries until mid-May, prepare for a surge in energy – and at the very least, for sparks to fly.

The Taurean New Moon on May 4th will be an ideal time to re-invent yourself and your ideas if you feel circumstances have grown stale. What's more, in mid-May your sign's ruler, Venus, will enter your own sign. Romance could blossom over coming weeks. Your values may change. The arts, music and romance are likely to appeal more than usual, so ensure you indulge in the areas of life you love the most.

And the Scorpio Full Moon on the 18th will further add to the idea that self-transformation is possible in May.

feminine energie?

MONDAY 22   ●

Sun conjunct Uranus and Venus semi-sextile Uranus: a surprise or a change of circumstance is on the way; love could blossom. Moon in Sagittarius.

TUESDAY 23   ●

Moon enters Capricorn.

WEDNESDAY 24   ●

Pluto turns retrograde: you may re-think a long-term development over coming weeks. Moon in Capricorn.

THURSDAY 25   ●

Moon in Capricorn.

FRIDAY 26   ☾

Moon enters Aquarius.

SATURDAY 27   ☾

Mars square Neptune: Avoid misunderstandings; someone may seem vague.
Have you romanticized an event? Avoid mislaying belongings.
Moon in Aquarius.

SUNDAY 28   ☾

Moon enters Pisces.

			APRIL			
S	M	T	W	T	F	S
	1	2	3	4	5	6
7	8	9	10	11	12	13
14	15	16	17	18	19	20
21	22	23	24	25	26	27
28	29	30				

MONDAY 29 ☾

Saturn turns retrograde: a good time to do a work check and ensure you're on track work-wise. Moon in Pisces.

TUESDAY 30 ☾

Moon in Pisces.

WEDNESDAY 1 ☾

Mercury sextile Mars; Mercury square Saturn; Mercury square Moon's Nodes; Saturn conjunct Moon's South Node: communications and research should be busy; information comes to light. Avoid impulsiveness and stubbornness, but keep an eye out for news. Remember: you can't agree with everyone. A reunion may appeal or you may meet an influential person. Moon enters Aries.

THURSDAY 2 ☾

Mercury square Pluto; Mercury trine Jupiter: another busy day for communications. Avoid conflict, as it may be long-standing. Avoid exaggeration. Travel and visitors may be significant. Good news or a productive trip could be on the way. Moon in Aries.

TAURUS

FRIDAY 3 (

Moon enters Taurus.

SATURDAY 4 ○

New Moon in Taurus: turn a page in your personal life, especially Taureans and Scorpios. Boost self-esteem and self-worth.

SUNDAY 5)

Moon in Taurus.

may 1-11 use
your mind wisely!
(take heart out of it)
and intuition
Believe in yourself
Time to heal
3 55   overcome any obstcle

		MAY				
S	M	T	W	T	F	S
			1	2	3	4
5	6	7	8	9	10	11
12	13	14	15	16	17	18
19	20	21	22	23	24	25
26	27	28	29	30	31	

MONDAY 6)

Mercury enters Taurus; Venus square Moon's Nodes: you may question your values or those of someone else; communications should even out. It's a good time to put practical ideas in words and on paper over the next few weeks. Moon enters Gemini.

TUESDAY 7)

Venus square Saturn: a serious commitment can be made, but check your values are supported. An authority figure may have news. Moon in Gemini.

WEDNESDAY 8)

Mercury conjunct Uranus: you may receive unexpected news or must change your routine from out of the blue. You may bump into an old friend. Moon enters Cancer.

THURSDAY 9)

Venus trine Jupiter; Venus square Pluto: you may feel conflicted in your feelings. You'll be attracted to music, dance and art, but someone may have intense feelings. You'll feel motivated to get ahead, but must avoid excesses and conflict. Moon in Cancer.

FRIDAY 10 ☽

Moon enters Leo.

SATURDAY 11 ☽

Sun trine Saturn: your efforts will be rewarded. A great day to get plans underway and to make agreements. Moon in Leo.

SUNDAY 12 ☽

Moon enters Virgo.

		MAY				
S	M	T	W	T	F	S
			1	2	3	4
5	6	7	8	9	10	11
12	13	14	15	16	17	18
19	20	21	22	23	24	25
26	27	28	29	30	31	

MONDAY 13 ●

Moon in Virgo.

TUESDAY 14 ●

Venus sextile Mars; Sun trine Pluto: a good day to get ahead with plans to change areas of your life or ideas that can lead to self-improvement. Put plans in place to gradually transform your life. Your plans should show progress; take the initiative. Romance could blossom. Moon enters Libra.

WEDNESDAY 15 ●

Venus enters Taurus: Romance should blossom over coming weeks. Your values may change. The arts, music and romance may appeal more than usual. Moon in Libra.

THURSDAY 16 ●

Mars enters Cancer; Mercury sextile Neptune: Mercury trine Saturn: practical decisions can be made today; ensure you research agreements. Work and communications could be successful. Your plans may take a fresh turn. Moon enters Scorpio.

FRIDAY 17 ●

Moon in Scorpio.

SATURDAY 18 ●

Full Moon in Scorpio; Mercury trine Pluto: conversations should go well, but if you feel you're being railroaded, take your time to consider options. A passionate time: self-transformation is possible now.

SUNDAY 19 ●

Moon enters Sagittarius.

			MAY			
S	M	T	W	T	F	S
			1	2	3	4
5	6	7	8	9	10	11
12	13	14	15	16	17	18
19	20	21	22	23	24	25
26	27	28	29	30	31	

MAY TO JUNE 2019

Sun enters Gemini, May 21st

How ready are you to move ahead with exciting projects – and which considerations would hold you back? If you are sentimental or nostalgic, this month's events may pull at your heart strings and you may be inclined to cling to the past or to tried-and-trusted routines you have subscribed to for many months if not years.

But if you're a pioneer and ready to experience new projects and exciting opportunities, and to advance and to grow in your journey, this month will be an exciting turning point for you.

Bear in mind that in July the eclipses will spur you on into new circumstances regardless of your mindset, so be prepared to move ahead and to adapt to the new, whether you want it or not.

The Gemini New Moon on June 3rd will be conducive to research, to paperwork and to communications where you already have an inkling that things are about to change – and where you're already in the midst of change. And, with Mercury in Cancer from June 5th to the 27th, the more you use your intuition, the better for you.

Mercury in Cancer is an excellent time for introspection, and to learn meditation and to study metaphysics, for example. Hone your instincts during this phase as you will benefit from being able to trust your intuition, especially as the eclipses in July will ask that you think on your feet.

Once Venus is in Gemini (from June 9th to July 2nd), you'll appreciate the groundswell of energy that promises more adaptability and flexibility in your life, and that prepares you for changes to come.

The Sagittarian Full Moon on June 17th will spotlight an adventurous plan – and notably how realistic and practical it is. If you have built castles in the air you are likely to find out at this time, and disappointing as it may be, nevertheless, it will enable you to make the necessary changes for a steadier path ahead.

For Geminis:

The Gemini New Moon on June 3rd will coincide with a beautiful Venus-Pluto alignment, suggesting this is the time to take action in areas where you wish to see change, especially in your love life, profile and finances. The more sensitive you are not only to others' needs but also to your own, the more you will progress in the areas you wish to generate success in, especially financially and at home. Key news to do with home, self-development and/or a property could signal a fresh chapter ahead.

The entire month of June is ideal for you to work with groups, friends and organizations, and to network in general, especially if you wish to introduce a new skill or aspect of yourself. This is the month where you could manage to put yourself in a new or a more positive light.

Agreements you make around the Sagittarian Full Moon on June 17th could signal exciting times ahead, where you will feel you are in a position to follow a dream. So don't hesitate to consider new ventures at this time, especially if you have already planned ahead or dreamed about fabulous and progressive developments in the past.

MONDAY 20

Moon in Sagittarius.

TUESDAY 21

Sun and Mercury enter Gemini; Sun conjunct Mercury: there will be more focus on communications and networking, finances and business, over coming weeks. News or a trip may be significant today. Moon enters Capricorn.

WEDNESDAY 22

Mars sextile Uranus: an unexpected or delightful event. Moon in Capricorn.

THURSDAY 23

Mercury sextile Chiron: news could involve healing matters; a trip may be therapeutic. Moon enters Aquarius.

FRIDAY 24 ◖

Mars square Chiron: avoid impulsiveness; a good day for health appointments. Moon in Aquarius.

SATURDAY 25 ◖

Sun semi-sextile Uranus: a surprise may arise. Moon in Aquarius.

SUNDAY 26 ◖

Moon enters Pisces.

			MAY			
S	M	T	W	T	F	S
			1	2	3	4
5	6	7	8	9	10	11
12	13	14	15	16	17	18
19	20	21	22	23	24	25
26	27	28	29	30	31	

MONDAY 27 ☽

Moon in Pisces.

TUESDAY 28 ☽

Moon enters Aries.

WEDNESDAY 29 ☽

Mercury semi-sextile Venus: a good day to talk. Moon in Aries.

THURSDAY 30 ☽

Venus sextile Neptune: art, romance, beauty and dance will all appeal.
Moon in Aries.

FRIDAY 31   (

*Mercury opposite Jupiter; Venus trine Saturn: a good day to make practical
agreements and plans and for romance, as long as you're realistic and
keep conversations on an even keel, as you may be prone to indecision and
misunderstandings. Moon enters Taurus.*

SATURDAY 1   (

Moon in Taurus.

SUNDAY 2   (

Moon enters Gemini.

			MAY			
S	M	T	W	T	F	S
			1	2	3	4
5	6	7	8	9	10	11
12	13	14	15	16	17	18
19	20	21	22	23	24	25
26	27	28	29	30	31	

MONDAY 3 ○

New Moon in Gemini: a fresh understanding or communications device may appeal. Venus trine Pluto: your plans could take a step forward. Love may blossom, but you must avoid intense topics.

TUESDAY 4)

Mercury enters Cancer: a more intuitive way to communicate may appeal over coming weeks. Moon enters Cancer.

WEDNESDAY 5)

Moon in Cancer.

THURSDAY 6)

Moon enters Leo.

FRIDAY 7   ❭

Mercury sextile Uranus: expect an unusual or out-of-the-ordinary event or news. A good day for meetings. Moon in Leo.

SATURDAY 8   ❭

Moon enters Virgo.

SUNDAY 9   ❭

Venus enters Gemini; Sun square Neptune: you may find value in new areas in life over the coming weeks, so keep an open mind and try something new! Avoid overindulgence and misunderstandings. Moon in Virgo.

JUNE

S	M	T	W	T	F	S
						1
2	3	4	5	6	7	8
9	10	11	12	13	14	15
16	17	18	19	20	21	22
23	24	25	26	27	28	29
30						

MONDAY 10 ◗

Sun opposite Jupiter: you may feel restless or undecided. Allow reason to triumph over emotions in business, but let passions reign in love and art! Moon in Virgo.

TUESDAY 11 ◗

Moon enters Libra.

WEDNESDAY 12 ◗

Mars conjunct Moon's North Node: someone special may come to your attention. Avoid acting impulsively. Moon in Libra.

THURSDAY 13 ●

Venus semi-sextile Uranus; Venus sextile Chiron: a healing or therapeutic event may come from out of the blue or may be out of the ordinary. A good day to mend bridges. Moon enters Scorpio.

FRIDAY 14 ●

Mars trine Neptune; Mars opposite Saturn: you may be led by your passions.
You may be asked to stick to certain rules. Moon in Scorpio.

SATURDAY 15 ●

Moon enters Sagittarius.

SUNDAY 16 ●

Mercury trine Neptune; Mercury opposite Saturn; Jupiter square Neptune:
you may be adventurous and bold, but certain boundaries may prevent
you from moving forward. You can succeed through research and by being
practical. Moon in Sagittarius.

			JUNE			
S	M	T	W	T	F	S
						1
2	3	4	5	6	7	8
9	10	11	12	13	14	15
16	17	18	19	20	21	22
23	24	25	26	27	28	29
30						

JUNE TO JULY 2019

Sun enters Cancer, June 21st

As the Sun enters Cancer this marks the summer solstice in the northern hemisphere, the longest day of the year. This is when seeds that have been sown, blossom, and farmers prepare for the harvest in September. The next four weeks are an ideal time to consider where you see your projects in three months' time, especially as the eclipses in July will bring change your way.

Mercury in Cancer until June 26th and Mars in Cancer until July 1st will ask that you use your intuition and navigate at this instinctive level, especially if you feel lost occasionally during this eventful time. However, Mars in Cancer can predispose those who are action-oriented and practical to feel a little drained in energy or even as though you are in deep water. Tune in to your intuition during this phase and the direction you gain from this invaluable internal compass will counteract the lack of energy and in fact will save you energy as you will avoid taking unnecessary action.

The total solar eclipse in Cancer on July 2nd will ask also that you consider the topic of nurturance – not only of self, but also of others. Where do you derive the greatest sense of support, and how do you reciprocate?

Luckily, with both Mercury and Mars in Leo in July until July 20th, your actions should become more easily expedited, especially until July 7th. After this time Mercury will be retrograde, giving you the opportunity to review some of your communications and ideas up until this time.

The partial lunar eclipse in Capricorn on July 16th will align with Pluto, suggesting key changes. And, with a Venus-Saturn opposition the next day, important decisions will be on the table; these may feel intense or simply challenging.

There is a sense of destiny this month, which may be attractive or it may be a trial. In the love stakes, there will be certain people you were always destined to meet; it's your choice now whether their significance in your life grows, or whether you move in a new direction.

For Cancerians:

The Moon's North Node is travelling through your sign this year, making this a year where you can deepen your understanding of your soul purpose. If you are unsure what your purpose is (other than to be true to yourself; a shining example and compassionate) this is the perfect time to investigate a little more about what – and who – really does create a sense of accomplishment in your life.

The total solar eclipse in your sign on July 2nd will coincide with an alignment between Saturn and the Moon's Nodes, pointing to a fated or pre-destined connection, especially if your birthday is early July. A commitment could be made – or broken. The Sun will then align with the Moon's North Node on July 10th, signifying once more key meetings or get-togethers that may be more relevant than meets the eye.

This phase will also be an ideal time to delve deeply into your own inner recesses to find out just what – and who – means the most to you in life right now, and what you will do to change your routine so you can fit more activities in line with your purpose in your daily life.

MONDAY 17 ●

Full Moon in Sagittarius: This is an excellent time to consider how you might see your plans in a more adventurous light; how communications could be more upbeat and how you may be more positive. Developments to do with travel, legal matters, study and spirituality are on the way.

TUESDAY 18 ●

Saturn sextile Neptune: agreements can be made today.
Moon enters Capricorn.

WEDNESDAY 19 ●

Mercury conjunct Mars; Mercury opposite Pluto: an important decision or conversation today may bring intense emotions to the surface. Be practical.
Moon in Capricorn.

THURSDAY 20 ●

Mars opposite Pluto: Avoid impulsive decisions, as intense developments could signal change. A good day to put changes in motion if you'd like swift progress.
Moon enters Aquarius.

FRIDAY 21

Sun enters Cancer. Summer solstice: time to celebrate life and look ahead at personal growth. Moon in Aquarius.

SATURDAY 22

Moon enters Pisces.

SUNDAY 23

Venus opposite Jupiter: not everyone will agree with you, but your plans could take a step forward. Love may blossom, but you must avoid intense conflict. Moon in Pisces.

		JUNE				
S	M	T	W	T	F	S
						1
2	3	4	5	6	7	8
9	10	11	12	13	14	15
16	17	18	19	20	21	22
23	24	25	26	27	28	29
30						

MONDAY 24   ☽

Venus square Neptune: you may be artistically inspired, but could let your imagination run away with you. Moon in Pisces.

TUESDAY 25   ☽

Moon enters Aries.

WEDNESDAY 26   ☽

Moon in Aries.

THURSDAY 27   ☽

Mercury enters Leo: communications may become more positive and upbeat for the next week. Sun sextile Uranus: expect the unexpected! A surprise is on the way. Moon enters Taurus.

FRIDAY 28 ☽

Moon in Taurus.

SATURDAY 29 ☽

Moon enters Gemini.

SUNDAY 30 ☽

Moon in Gemini.

		JUNE				
S	M	T	W	T	F	S
						1
2	3	4	5	6	7	8
9	10	11	12	13	14	15
16	17	18	19	20	21	22
23	24	25	26	27	28	29
30						

MONDAY 1   (

Mars enters Leo: Energy levels could pick up over the coming weeks, but watch out for feistiness. Moon in Gemini.

TUESDAY 2   ○

Total solar eclipse in Cancer: developments at home, to do with family or property, esoteric or spiritual matters, will gain your attention.

WEDNESDAY 3   )

Venus enters Cancer: your attention may turn towards home, nurturance and the importance of caring. Moon in Cancer.

THURSDAY 4   )

Moon's North Node opposite Saturn: an event or meeting may seem inevitable or involve rules and regulations and the chance to build more stability. Moon enters Leo.

FRIDAY 5)

Venus semi-sextile Mars: you may be led by your desires today. Meetings could be ideal. Moon in Leo.

SATURDAY 6)

Moon enters Virgo.

SUNDAY 7)

Mercury turns retrograde: you may be inclined to review and to revise your ideas until the end of the month. Avoid impulsive decisions during this time. Moon in Virgo.

			JULY			
S	M	T	W	T	F	S
	1	2	3	4	5	6
7	8	9	10	11	12	13
14	15	16	17	18	19	20
21	22	23	24	25	26	27
28	29	30	31			

MONDAY 8

Mercury conjunct Mars; Venus sextile Uranus; Chiron turns retrograde: you may receive key news today, some may surprise you. It's a good day to talk and to decide upon health issues. This will be an ideal time to research and to invest in your own health and wellbeing (until early December). Moon enters Libra.

TUESDAY 9

Sun opposite Saturn: key decisions may be made today. Moon in Libra.

WEDNESDAY 10

Sun conjunct North Node: a significant meeting could be fated or will mean more to you than meets the eye. Moon enters Scorpio.

THURSDAY 11

Sun trine Neptune; Mars square Uranus; Mars trine Chiron: a lovely day for romance, healing, the arts, spirituality and all things beautiful. You may feel idealistic, so keep your feet on the ground and avoid impulsiveness. Expect the unexpected. Moon in Scorpio.

FRIDAY 12 ●

Moon enters Sagittarius.

SATURDAY 13 ●

Moon in Sagittarius.

SUNDAY 14 ●

Sun opposite Pluto: events may feel intense today; avoid conflict as it may escalate. Moon in Sagittarius.

		JULY				
S	M	T	W	T	F	S
	1	2	3	4	5	6
7	8	9	10	11	12	13
14	15	16	17	18	19	20
21	22	23	24	25	26	27
28	29	30	31			

MONDAY 15 ●

Moon enters Capricorn.

TUESDAY 16 ●

Partial lunar eclipse in Capricorn: this may be an intense eclipse as it aligns with Pluto. Key changes to the way you consider work, authority figures, duties and nurturance may arise.

WEDNESDAY 17 ●

Venus opposite Saturn: key decisions can be made. An important meeting may arise. Look 'outside the square'. Moon enters Aquarius.

THURSDAY 18 ●

Venus conjunct North Node; Venus trine Neptune: you may meet someone close or someone you are strongly drawn to. Romance could blossom. Moon in Aquarius.

FRIDAY 19

Retrograde Mercury enters Cancer: matters to do with your home, domestic life, property or family may be up for review. Moon enters Pisces.

SATURDAY 20

Moon in Pisces.

SUNDAY 21

Sun conjunct Mercury; Venus opposite Pluto: key news may produce intense feelings. Romance may appeal. Moon in Pisces.

			JULY			
S	M	T	W	T	F	S
	1	2	3	4	5	6
7	8	9	10	11	12	13
14	15	16	17	18	19	20
21	22	23	24	25	26	27
28	29	30	31			

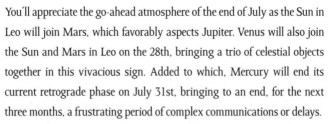

JULY TO AUGUST 2019

Sun enters Leo, July 23rd

You'll appreciate the go-ahead atmosphere of the end of July as the Sun in Leo will join Mars, which favorably aspects Jupiter. Venus will also join the Sun and Mars in Leo on the 28th, bringing a trio of celestial objects together in this vivacious sign. Added to which, Mercury will end its current retrograde phase on July 31st, bringing to an end, for the next three months, a frustrating period of complex communications or delays.

The Leo New Moon and Supermoon on August 1st will align with healing aspects from Chiron, the planet-asteroid called the 'Wounded Healer', associated with health, teaching, therapy and wellbeing. This New Moon is ideal for focussing on self-healing and study. A retreat, therapeutic study or self-healing modality may appeal at this time, and could be super successful. If you work in the medical or teaching professions, you may be particularly busy.

If key news arrives at the start of August, this may draw on your inner reserves. You may be ready to move forward in August with exciting new plans, with the benefit of fresh information.

August is likely to be busy, as there is also an upbeat vibe, especially during the week of August 7th to 15th, when you should enjoy all that life has to offer.

August 7th to 8th could be particularly enjoyable, so plan for exciting events then. And the dates around August 11th may bring considerable progress, when a change of routine or fresh developments bring fresh dynamics your way. You may be inclined to see the romance in life more at this time, making this ideal for self-development, uplifting events such as travel and learning and fun activities such as music, dance and romance.

A particularly healing or growing curve may peak around August 15th, and you may be surprised by the outcome of your hard work over the following days.

For Leos:

Nurturance is the key word for this phase and you will benefit greatly by following your hunches with regard to healthy and uplifting schedules that can boost your wellbeing. Both the New Moon Supermoon on August 1st and the Full Moon on August 15th will involve aspects to Chiron – the New Moon itself aspecting Chiron favorably; and Mercury on the 15th aspecting Chiron favorably. This suggests healing and self-help, and the propensity for advancement in spiritual ways will be a theme at this time.

For some, this may involve circumstances that mean you must recuperate; for example, you may choose to take time out because you are exhausted. For others though, this time will be ideal for delving into healing and spiritual studies so that you learn more fully and completely your own nurturing and healing abilities.

The week of August 7th to 15th will be particularly transformative. Plan to enjoy the activities you love most, then. And, if life serves an ultimatum, or you simply find adapting to circumstances mid-August is a little tricky, trust your instincts, pace yourself and remember: it's all about nurturance at the moment: of yourself, of others and of your environment.

Let your inner light shine and make affirmations to boost relationships around the Full Moon on August 15th.

MONDAY 22 ◖

Moon enters Aries.

TUESDAY 23 ◖

Sun enters Leo: prepare to feel more expressive and to let your inner light shine. Moon in Aries.

WEDNESDAY 24 ◖

Moon enters Taurus.

THURSDAY 25 ◖

Mercury conjunct Venus; Mars trine Jupiter: a good day to talk. Listen to your instincts. Avoid power plays and impulsiveness. Moon in Taurus.

FRIDAY 26   (

Moon in Taurus.

SATURDAY 27   (

Moon enters Gemini.

SUNDAY 28   (

Venus enters Leo: you may feel bolder, especially in love and money stakes, over the coming three weeks. Moon in Gemini.

			JULY			
S	M	T	W	T	F	S
	1	2	3	4	5	6
7	8	9	10	11	12	13
14	15	16	17	18	19	20
21	22	23	24	25	26	27
28	29	30	31			

MONDAY 29 (

Sun square Uranus; Sun trine Chiron: expect the unexpected; a sudden change of mind or of circumstance may occur. This could be a healing day.
Moon enters Cancer.

TUESDAY 30 (

Moon in Cancer.

WEDNESDAY 31 (

Moon enters Leo.

THURSDAY 1 ○

New Moon and Supermoon in Leo; Venus trine Chiron; Mercury ends a retrograde phase: communications should improve over time, although key news may arrive today. A trip may be more relevant than meets the eye: be ready to view a relationship or valued activity in a new light; a difficulty can be overcome. This is a good time to consider an exciting project.

FRIDAY 2 ⟩

Venus square Uranus: someone may surprise you; a routine may change.
Moon enters Virgo.

SATURDAY 3 ⟩

Moon in Virgo.

SUNDAY 4 ⟩

Moon enters Libra.

		AUGUST				
S	M	T	W	T	F	S
				1	2	3
4	5	6	7	8	9	10
11	12	13	14	15	16	17
18	19	20	21	22	23	24
25	26	27	28	29	30	31

MONDAY 5 ☽

Mars quincunx Pluto: avoid quarrels, they may escalate. A hurdle can be overcome. Moon in Libra.

TUESDAY 6 ☽

Moon enters Scorpio.

WEDNESDAY 7 ☽

Sun trine Jupiter: potentially a lucky break or upbeat news is on the way. Avoid excesses. Moon in Scorpio.

THURSDAY 8 ☽

Venus trine Jupiter: love and romance could blossom, but you may be easily influenced. Developments may gain their own momentum.
Moon enters Sagittarius.

FRIDAY 9 ◗

Venus quincunx Saturn: a hurdle and delays can be overcome.
Moon in Sagittarius.

SATURDAY 10 ◗

Moon in Sagittarius.

SUNDAY 11 ◗

Mercury enters Leo; Sun quincunx Neptune; Jupiter ends a retrograde phase;
Uranus turns retrograde: communications could be busy. You may be prone to
excesses and to being easily influenced; check the facts first.
Moon enters Capricorn.

| | | AUGUST | | | | |
S	M	T	W	T	F	S
				1	2	3
4	5	6	7	8	9	10
11	12	13	14	15	16	17
18	19	20	21	22	23	24
25	26	27	28	29	30	31

MONDAY 12

Moon in Capricorn.

TUESDAY 13

Moon enters Aquarius.

WEDNESDAY 14

Sun and Venus quincunx Pluto: you can come to a resolution even if matters are intense. Moon in Aquarius.

THURSDAY 15

Full Moon in Aquarius; Mercury trine Chiron: consider a fresh look or outlook. An excellent day to make changes in your health and wellbeing. You may receive good news. You must avoid impulsiveness.

FRIDAY 16 ●

Mercury square Uranus: unexpected events may occur. Avoid misunderstandings and delays by planning ahead. Moon enters Pisces.

SATURDAY 17 ●

Moon in Pisces.

SUNDAY 18 ●

Mars enters Virgo: you may feel motivated to get better organized and to boost health. Virgos may feel more energetic over the coming weeks.
Moon enters Aries.

			AUGUST			
S	M	T	W	T	F	S
				1	2	3
4	5	6	7	8	9	10
11	12	13	14	15	16	17
18	19	20	21	22	23	24
25	26	27	28	29	30	31

AUGUST TO
SEPTEMBER 2019

Sun enters Virgo, August 23rd

The day after the Sun enters Virgo, the sign associated with earthiness, service and methodology, a beautiful alignment between Venus and Mars will take all the focus from practicalities to romance. In fact, the final week of August will be a creative, idyllic time, when your imagination may run riot. So there is much merit in finding balance and 'earthing' yourself in this down-to-earth phase while the sun is in Virgo.

The Virgo New Moon and Supermoon on August 30th will give wings to the idea that we can be firmly rooted in earth and our material existence, while still being inspired by spiritual and lofty ideas. And that, in fact, the better you combine your practical, earthy side with your spiritual endeavors, the more effectively you will manifest your spiritual ideas.

In September, Venus, Mercury, the Sun and then Mars will align opposite Neptune, and these aspects will heighten spiritual endeavours, but may also predispose you to absent-mindedness and daydreaming. All the more reason to remain firmly earthed and practical.

Added to which, the Pisces Full Moon on September 14th will create a sense of wonder and idealism. At this time, if you do not combine practicalities with realism and method, you risk being illogical and could make mistakes. If you are predisposed to addictions, such as drug dependency, watch out as this phase could set you back if you've already embarked on a healing treatment.

The key to success this month will be your diligence and sense of purpose even if you feel lost or lose your sense of direction. Avoid being disappointed if you feel lost; it's often in this way that you get back on track. It's in the searching that you'll find true gems.

For Virgos:

There is an opportunity for adventure and excitement over the next four months. That is, if you can stick with a clever plan and avoid going off-path. With three planets and the Sun in your sign from the end of August until mid-September, there's every potential that you make a dream come true. But because these planets align opposite Neptune, there's equal potential that you make mistakes, misjudge your circumstances or, worse, lose your way.

Luckily, a fortunate aspect between the Sun and the Moon's North Node, Saturn and Pluto will encourage you to be practical and stick with truly transformative plans, leading to a sense of accomplishment.

The Virgo New Moon and Supermoon on August 30th will encourage you to focus on your wellbeing, vitality and ability to reinvent yourself. This is the time to initiate new projects – with the proviso that you've adequately researched your circumstances and push forward with facts and information at your fingertips.

Keep an eye out around the Full Moon in Pisces on September 14th: you could make a dream come true as long as you base your actions on clever planning and realistic information. And, if you discover you have made an error towards September 21st to 22nd, consider this as a godsend: the fact you've discovered the mistake means you can put things right.

MONDAY 19

Moon in Aries.

TUESDAY 20

Moon in Aries.

WEDNESDAY 21

Mercury trine Jupiter: Venus enters Virgo: focus on beauty, wellbeing, health and fitness will pep up your daily routine. A good time to get organizsed. Good news or a productive trip could be on the way. Moon enters Taurus.

THURSDAY 22

Moon in Taurus.

FRIDAY 23   (

Sun enters Virgo: time to focus on health, wellbeing, work and being helpful over the next few weeks. This may be a varied day. Moon enters Gemini.

SATURDAY 24   (

Venus conjunct Mars: love and romance could flourish. An indulgent day. Investments may appeal. Check details. Moon in Gemini.

SUNDAY 25   (

Venus quincunx Chiron: a good day for health appointments. Avoid taking random comments personally. Moon enters Cancer.

AUGUST

S	M	T	W	T	F	S
				1	2	3
4	5	6	7	8	9	10
11	12	13	14	15	16	17
18	19	20	21	22	23	24
25	26	27	28	29	30	31

MONDAY 26 (

Venus trine Uranus: you may be surprised by events today. You can put change in motion now. Moon in Cancer.

TUESDAY 27 (

Moon in Cancer.

WEDNESDAY 28 (

Mars trine Uranus: a motivational day; you may make rapid progress, but may also be surprised by events. Moon enters Leo.

THURSDAY 29 (

Mercury enters Virgo; Sun trine Uranus: you may experience a surprise today; events may gain momentum. An unexpected event should delight. You should experience improved communications over the following weeks, especially Virgos and Pisces. Moon in Leo.

FRIDAY 30 ○

New Moon and Supermoon in Virgo: an inspiring time to get ship-shape and healthy and spruce up a fresh work routine.

SATURDAY 31)

Moon in Virgo.

SUNDAY 1)

Mercury trine Uranus; Venus trine Saturn: you could make great headway today with change you'd like to implement. Moon enters Libra.

		AUGUST				
S	M	T	W	T	F	S
				1	2	3
4	5	6	7	8	9	10
11	12	13	14	15	16	17
18	19	20	21	22	23	24
25	26	27	28	29	30	31

MONDAY 2)

Sun conjunct Mars; Venus square Jupiter: you could accomplish a great deal today. Avoid rash decisions; you may need to temper strong emotions. Check your values and priorities. Someone may seem feisty. Moon in Libra.

TUESDAY 3)

Mercury conjunct Mars; Mercury conjunct the Sun: you or someone close may behave uncharacteristically rash. Think before you speak. News may be unexpected. Moon enters Scorpio.

WEDNESDAY 4)

Venus opposite Neptune: art, music, romance and dance will appeal. Someone's viewpoints may differ from yours. Beauty in its many forms will appeal. You may be forgetful, or nostalgic. Moon in Scorpio.

THURSDAY 5)

Mercury trine Saturn: a good day to talk and to make agreements and plans. Moon enters Sagittarius.

FRIDAY 6

Sun trine Saturn; Mercury square Jupiter: your views may differ from someone else's. Boost self-esteem and take practical steps to implement clever plans. Avoid: misunderstandings and arrogance; plan ahead to avoid delays. Moon in Sagittarius.

SATURDAY 7

Mercury opposite Neptune: avoid delays by planning ahead. Avoid absentmindedness and misunderstandings. Romance and enjoyable ventures will appeal. Ensure your facts are straight. Moon enters Capricorn.

SUNDAY 8

Sun square Jupiter: your wishes may clash with someone else's. Optimism may pay off. Set your sights realistically. Moon in Capricorn.

		SEPTEMBER				
S	M	T	W	T	F	S
1	2	3	4	5	6	7
8	9	10	11	12	13	14
15	16	17	18	19	20	21
22	23	24	25	26	27	28
29	30					

MONDAY 9 ●

Mercury trine Pluto; Mars trine Saturn: talks may be busy today; you can achieve a great deal, but you must focus on practicalities and realities. Moon enters Aquarius.

TUESDAY 10 ●

Sun opposite Neptune: you may feel idealistic today. Romance could blossom; your interest in art, film and music will flourish. Moon in Aquarius.

WEDNESDAY 11 ●

Moon in Aquarius.

THURSDAY 12 ●

Mars square Jupiter: you could attain an important goal if you avoid impulsiveness. Moon enters Pisces.

FRIDAY 13   ●

Friday 13th! Mercury conjunct Venus; Sun trine Pluto: a good day to talk about love, money and priorities. You could make considerable changes now. Romance is on the cards. Avoid impulsiveness. Moon in Pisces.

SATURDAY 14   ●

Full Moon in Pisces; Mars opposite Neptune; Mercury and Venus enter Libra: you could make a dream come true as long as you base your actions on clever planning and real information. Moon enters Aries in the evening.

SUNDAY 15   ●

Moon in Aries.

		SEPTEMBER				
S	M	T	W	T	F	S
1	2	3	4	5	6	7
8	9	10	11	12	13	14
15	16	17	18	19	20	21
22	23	24	25	26	27	28
29	30					

MONDAY 16 ●

Moon in Aries.

TUESDAY 17 ●

Mercury quincunx Uranus: you may be surprised by news.
Moon enters Taurus.

WEDNESDAY 18 ●

Saturn ends a retrograde phase: work, your duties, plans and responsibilities
should be easier to complete over the coming weeks and months.
Moon in Taurus.

THURSDAY 19 ◖

Moon enters Gemini.

FRIDAY 20 ◖

Moon in Gemini.

SATURDAY 21 ◖

Jupiter square Neptune: you may discover a secret, or new information.
Moon in Gemini.

SUNDAY 22 ◖

*Mercury square Saturn: you may be called upon to be responsible or to make
a commitment. If you encounter an obstacle, see it as a reality check. Avoid:
misunderstandings. Moon enters Cancer.*

		SEPTEMBER				
S	M	T	W	T	F	S
1	2	3	4	5	6	7
8	9	10	11	12	13	14
15	16	17	18	19	20	21
22	23	24	25	26	27	28
29	30					

SEPTEMBER TO OCTOBER 2019

Sun enters Libra, September 23rd

This is the time of year to look for harmony and balance in life. The entry of the Sun into Libra marks the Autumn equinox in the northern hemisphere, when the day is almost equal to night, bringing a desire for balance to mind as we head towards winter. What's more, the New Moon and Supermoon in Libra on September 28th will further accentuate the sense that balance, a fair go and justice have a place in your life.

As Pluto, the planet astrologers associate with transformation, will end a lengthy five-month retrograde phase on October 3rd, you'll increasingly gain the sense over the coming months that the changes you wish to make in your life will become more viable. Those changes will begin to take effect much more readily as the year progresses.

And, with Mercury in Libra until October 4th, and Mars in Libra from October 4th, communications will tend to revolve around the need to seek balance, agreement and harmony in life. You may find yourself in the position of negotiator or mediator, or needing a mediator yourself to settle disagreements from time to time. Contracts and collaborations could be significant.

Your communications and interactions may become a little intense for the rest of October, with Mercury in Scorpio from October 5th onwards.

Therefore, do your checks and balances to ensure you're still consciously creating balance and harmony in your projects and relationships.

The Aries Full Moon on October 13th will be an excellent time to ensure you are happy with the direction your life is taking, as you will gain the insight to make changes at this time. This Full Moon will also highlight which relationships are supportive and which simply aren't. A desire for change may be insurmountable. The key to moving ahead will rest in careful planning, not impulsive decisions.

For Librans:

The Libran New Moon and Supermoon on September 28th will kick-start a fresh phase in which commitments – both in your personal life and at work – become a key motivator. Developments that occur in the next four weeks may be connected with events that occurred at the end of April/early May, and will point to significant contact with someone you seem to have a predestined connection with. The time is ripe to put in place healthier schedules. A trip or a visit may be significant at the New Moon, leading to new options further down the line.

The Aries Full Moon on October 13th will spotlight a partnership. Does this collaboration take you where you wish to be, or have you outgrown it? Is there still room for compassion, growth and mutual support? Honest conversation, negotiation and, for some, travel will be the turning points in relationships.

Positive planetary alignments will ask that you trust your intuition and avoid being easily led. It's time to stand strong and firm, and believe your strength and potential. With motivational Mars in Libra from October 4th to November 19th, you will have the power and the energy to get things done.

MONDAY 23 ☾

Sun enters Libra: autumn equinox; a time to integrate ideas, give thanks and prepare for winter. Look for balance and a fair go over the coming weeks. Moon in Cancer.

TUESDAY 24 ☾

Mercury sextile Jupiter: words will flow. You can make great headway with communications and travel plans. Moon enters Leo.

WEDNESDAY 25 ☾

Venus square Saturn: a serious commitment can be made, but check your values are supported. An authority figure may have news. Moon in Leo.

THURSDAY 26 ☾

Moon enters Virgo.

FRIDAY 27   (

Mercury square Pluto: you can excel, even under duress. Avoid obsessing over details; try to be flexible with changes in your routine. Your ideas may be challenged, or communications may be intense. Moon in Virgo.

SATURDAY 28   ○

New Moon and Supermoon in Libra; Saturn conjunct Moon's South Node: you may become aware of someone's vulnerability, even your own. Look for balance and a healthy routine, especially in relationships. If something or someone is holding you back, consider how to progress.

SUNDAY 29   )

Venus sextile Jupiter; Sun quincunx Uranus: a lovely day to arrange a creative event or to indulge in the arts, theatre and film. Romance could blossom. A surprise may arise; be innovative. Moon in Libra.

SEPTEMBER

S	M	T	W	T	F	S
1	2	3	4	5	6	7
8	9	10	11	12	13	14
15	16	17	18	19	20	21
22	23	24	25	26	27	28
29	30					

MONDAY 30   )

Moon enters Scorpio.

TUESDAY 1   )

Venus square Pluto: passions are likely to run high. You'll get ahead with considerable motivation, but must avoid excesses and conflict.
Moon in Scorpio.

WEDNESDAY 2   )

Moon enters Sagittarius.

THURSDAY 3   )

Mercury enters Scorpio; Pluto ends a retrograde phase: you'll feel more attuned to your instincts, emotions and desires over the coming weeks. You may even surprise yourself with some of your insights. A good time to communicate deep emotions, but avoid being super intense. It will become easier to implement changes. Moon in Sagittarius.

FRIDAY 4 ❍

*Mars enters Libra. Looking for and finding balance, fair-mindedness and
harmony in life will appeal over the coming weeks until mid-November.
Moon enters Capricorn.*

SATURDAY 5 ❍

Moon in Capricorn.

SUNDAY 6 ❍

Moon in Capricorn.

		OCTOBER				
S	M	T	W	T	F	S
		1	2	3	4	5
6	7	8	9	10	11	12
13	14	15	16	17	18	19
20	21	22	23	24	25	26
27	28	29	30	31		

MONDAY 7 ●

Mercury opposite Uranus: an unexpected change of plan, or surprise news may arise. Someone may behave unpredictably. Moon enters Aquarius.

TUESDAY 8 ●

Venus enters Scorpio; Mars opposite Chiron: passion, love and emotions will all bubble up over the coming weeks. Avoid being over-sensitive today; let emotions calm down. Moon in Aquarius.

WEDNESDAY 9 ●

Sun quincunx Neptune: you can overcome confusion or delays with careful planning. Moon enters Pisces.

THURSDAY 10 ●

Moon in Pisces.

FRIDAY 11   ●

Moon in Pisces.

SATURDAY 12   ●

Venus opposite Uranus; Mars quincunx Uranus: an unexpected event may arise. Avoid impulsiveness but be spontaneous. Someone – perhaps even you! – may change their mind. Moon enters Aries.

SUNDAY 13   ●

Full Moon in Aries; Sun sextile Jupiter: a dynamic time, avoid being hasty. Be bold and take the initiative. Find ways to adapt to change, especially if it is inevitable.

		OCTOBER				
S	M	T	W	T	F	S
		1	2	3	4	5
6	7	8	9	10	11	12
13	14	15	16	17	18	19
20	21	22	23	24	25	26
27	28	29	30	31		

MONDAY 14 ●

Mercury sextile Saturn; Sun square Pluto: use good communication skills and avoid conflict, as it is likely to escalate or to be long-standing. Aim to make agreements instead. Moon in Aries.

TUESDAY 15 ●

Mercury trine Neptune: a great day to tune into your instincts and to enjoy meditation and spiritual work. Let your inner artist out; a great day for writing, enjoyment of music and theatre. Moon enters Taurus.

WEDNESDAY 16 ●

Moon in Taurus.

THURSDAY 17 ●

Jupiter semi-sextile Pluto: change may be as advantageous as no change. Try to see your way forward without a battle of wills. Moon enters Gemini.

FRIDAY 18

Moon in Gemini.

SATURDAY 19

Mercury sextile Pluto: choose words carefully, and you could make changes you wish for. A trip could be transformational. Moon enters Cancer.

SUNDAY 20

Venus sextile Saturn: a good day to make agreements. Be realistic.
Moon in Cancer.

		OCTOBER				
S	M	T	W	T	F	S
		1	2	3	4	5
6	7	8	9	10	11	12
13	14	15	16	17	18	19
20	21	22	23	24	25	26
27	28	29	30	31		

OCTOBER TO NOVEMBER 2019

Sun enters Scorpio, October 23rd

Just as the Sun enters passionate Scorpio and spirits fire up, there will also be a lovely alignment between Venus and Pluto, which will stimulate romance, interest in art, self-improvement and self-transformation. The end of October really is a wonderful time to make space for your interests, especially those that involve the arts, self-improvement and spirituality.

And, if you're ready to act on inspiring ideas that could mean long-term change such as a move or a change of direction work-wise, the period October 27th to October 31st, will be an excellent time to put in motion cleverly made plans even if you must be adaptable as you implement your ideas.

The important factor associated with progress now will lie in avoiding clinging to the past merely for the sake of it; there will be reasons for moving forward if you are brave and trust your instincts.

You'll find November ideal for a little introspection; and also for spiritual development. Mercury retrograde in Scorpio until November 19th may also bring up past memories or insecurities, so ensure you take things step by step. During this time, if you have decided to make considerable changes in your life, you may find you must tie up loose ends.

Venus in Sagittarius for most of November will help you to embrace an adventurous new phase, even if your vulnerabilities arise early November.

The Taurus Full Moon on November 12th will help you feel you have made the right decisions. This Full Moon will be grounding and, if you require direction, will highlight where you can move forward in the most practical ways.

After November 20th, communications, negotiations and travel should become more fluid and flexible, and you should feel, if the changes you are making are challenging, that you have overcome the worst hurdles.

For Scorpios:

You'll enjoy pursuing interests that engage you on a fundamental, passionate level. The Scorpio New Moon on October 28th may highlight where you wish to make changes in your life; and where these have not as yet quite materialized. Now you'll have every opportunity to make these changes, especially regarding your love life, finances and values in general. Once Mercury is retrograde from October 31st until November 19th, this will be an excellent time to review exactly what – and who – is most important to you.

The Full Moon on November 12th will spotlight your passions, and you'll certainly enjoy celebrating your earthly desires. In fact a dreamy time during the second week in November may involve the chance to get away; more romance or simply the upbeat opportunity to include more of all the qualities you love in life.

Once Mars enters your sign on November 20th, where it will stay until early next year, you should feel revitalized and ready to take on life's challenges – and to enjoy its pleasures.

MONDAY 21   ◖

Venus trine Neptune: a lovely day for a get-together, especially romantically or involving the arts, music and dance. Moon enters Leo.

TUESDAY 22   ◖

Moon in Leo.

WEDNESDAY 23   ◖

Sun enters Scorpio: passion will ramp up over the coming weeks!
Moon enters Virgo.

THURSDAY 24   ◖

Moon in Virgo.

FRIDAY 25 (

Venus sextile Pluto: a lovely day for romance, art, self-improvement, a healthy treat. Moon enters Libra.

SATURDAY 26 (

Venus semi-sextile Jupiter; Sun quincunx Chiron: be optimistic and enjoy life. Keep persevering if at first you don't succeed. Avoid taking the random comments of other people personally. A day to focus on health and wellbeing. Avoid over-indulgence. Moon in Libra.

SUNDAY 27 (

Mars square Saturn: you must be prepared for hard work and to avoid impulsiveness. A surprise may arise. Moon enters Scorpio.

OCTOBER

S	M	T	W	T	F	S
		1	2	3	4	5
6	7	8	9	10	11	12
13	14	15	16	17	18	19
20	21	22	23	24	25	26
27	28	29	30	31		

MONDAY 28   ○

New Moon in Scorpio; Sun opposite Uranus: expect the unexpected. You may feel restless or indecisive, so take things step by step. Be spontaneous and enjoy life. A good time to make changes or to begin new projects, especially if these are long term or involve great transformation.

TUESDAY 29   )

Moon enters Sagittarius.

WEDNESDAY 30   )

Mercury conjunct Venus: key news arrives. A good day for a get-together and to make a decision. Moon in Sagittarius.

THURSDAY 31   )

Mercury begins a retrograde phase: news or developments may motivate you to re-think or to review your circumstances over the next three weeks. A trip to an old haunt may appeal. Avoid forgetfulness and overt idealism.
Moon in Sagittarius.

SCORPIO

FRIDAY 1   ☽

*Venus enters Sagittarius: you may experience a more upbeat phase in the love
stakes, and feel more adventurous in life. Moon enters Capricorn.*

SATURDAY 2   ☽

Moon in Capricorn.

SUNDAY 3   ☽

*Venus trine Chiron: you can mend bridges today. A healing day, especially for
the heart. Moon enters Aquarius.*

		OCTOBER				
S	M	T	W	T	F	S
		1	2	3	4	5
6	7	8	9	10	11	12
13	14	15	16	17	18	19
20	21	22	23	24	25	26
27	28	29	30	31		

MONDAY 4   ☽

Moon in Aquarius.

TUESDAY 5   ☽

Mars square Pluto: pressure could lead to success, but if you do feel stressed, find a way to relieve tension. Conflict could escalate, so look for solutions. Moon in Aquarius.

WEDNESDAY 6   ☽

Moon enters Pisces

THURSDAY 7   ●

Mercury semi-sextile Jupiter: a good day to consider financial and travel plans. Moon in Pisces.

FRIDAY 8 ●

Sun sextile Saturn; Sun trine Neptune: a good day to be inspired while also being practical. Moon enters Aries.

SATURDAY 9 ●

Saturn sextile Neptune: be practical with your inspired plans, and take action step by step. Moon in Aries.

SUNDAY 10 ●

Moon in Aries.

		NOVEMBER				
S	M	T	W	T	F	S
					1	2
3	4	5	6	7	8	9
10	11	12	13	14	15	16
17	18	19	20	21	22	23
24	25	26	27	28	29	30

MONDAY 11 ●

Sun conjunct Mercury: a good day for talks and for travel plans. News and talks should be upbeat. Avoid impulsiveness. Moon enters Taurus.

TUESDAY 12 ●

Full Moon in Taurus; Mars sextile Jupiter: an excellent time to get your feet on the ground and to enjoy life's delights and a little luxury. Avoid over-indulgence and impulsiveness; you'll regret it!

WEDNESDAY 13 ●

Mercury sextile Saturn; Sun sextile Pluto: a good day to review long-term plans and for talks with authority figures. Moon enters Gemini.

THURSDAY 14 ●

Mercury trine Neptune; Venus square Neptune: a great day to tune in to your instincts and to enjoy meditation and spiritual work. Your inner artist may rise up; a great day for writing and the enjoyment of music and theatre. Avoid forgetfulness and be practical. Moon in Gemini.

FRIDAY 15

Venus semi-sextile Saturn: a good day to get ahead at work and to organize finances. Moon enters Cancer.

SATURDAY 16

Moon in Cancer.

SUNDAY 17

Moon enters Leo.

		NOVEMBER				
S	M	T	W	T	F	S
					1	2
3	4	5	6	7	8	9
10	11	12	13	14	15	16
17	18	19	20	21	22	23
24	25	26	27	28	29	30

NOVEMBER TO
DECEMBER 2019

Sun enters Sagittarius, November 22nd

Just as the Sun enters Sagittarius it will align harmoniously with 'wounded healer' Chiron, the planet-asteroid associated with healing and teaching. This suggests that you will benefit over the coming four weeks by considering self-development via healing and study. And, as Mars simultaneously aligns opposite Uranus, this will help give you the motivation to get busy with exciting new plans and projects.

The Sagittarian New Moon on November 26th will coincide with the entry of Venus into Capricorn, suggesting that your wishes and desires will find material expression. So this will be an ideal New Moon for launching new ideas and projects, as you are likely to birth these in practical ways.

Jupiter will enter Capricorn on December 2nd, bringing an added sense of stability and potential as we collectively head towards the new year. Take the initiative to make practical changes in your life that are healthy, practical and serve a higher purpose.

Above all, ensure you are well-informed and allow inspiration to guide you but do not be misled by ideas that are simply pie in the sky.

The Gemini Full Moon on December 12th will provide ample opportunity to get paperwork and communications ship-shape, even if a decision seems pressing or simply brings up doubts into being. The Jupiter 'trine' aspect to Uranus on December 15th should bring the confirmation you need that your exciting plans are for the best. But if you're still in doubt, inform yourself of your options especially around December 20th when lingering doubts can be dispelled.

For Sagittarians:

With Venus in your sign until November 25th, love, money, friendship and values will be uppermost in your mind as you consider how best to sail forward in these key areas over the next four weeks.

Once your sign's ruler, Jupiter, steps into earthy Capricorn on December 2nd, your perspective may change about work, a particular person – or even your own interests. Avoid making impulsive decisions. Now is the time to earth and birth new ideas.

The Sagittarian New Moon on November 26th will be marvelous for initiating new projects, but if you feel your ideas or plans are opposed, consider how you might work to ultimately perfect your plans.

A domestic, property or spiritual matter may be best seen from the point of view of values and ultimate worth. For example, if you feel undervalued this is the time to start blowing your trumpet; if you feel property is overvalued, this is the time to look elsewhere.

Maintain positive expectations and optimism, and by December 16th you should see positive results for your hard work in all fields, especially your domestic arena.

MONDAY 18 ◀

Venus semi-sextile Pluto: a good day for health and beauty treats. A good day also to make changes, especially those that relate to romance. Moon in Leo.

TUESDAY 19 ◀

Mars enters Scorpio: a passionate phase will begin. You'll feel motivated to succeed. Moon in Leo.

WEDNESDAY 20 ◀

Mercury ends its retrograde phase: communications and travel may become easier if you've experienced delays or difficulties. Moon enters Virgo.

THURSDAY 21 ◖

Moon in Virgo.

FRIDAY 22   (

Sun enters Sagittarius: let your inner adventurer out over the coming weeks.
Moon enters Libra.

SATURDAY 23   (

Moon in Libra.

SUNDAY 24   (

Venus conjunct Jupiter; Sun trine Chiron; Mars opposite Uranus: you may be
inclined to follow your heart, but caution is warranted to avoid impulsiveness.
If you have prepared well, a dream could come true. A good day for healing.
Moon enters Scorpio.

		NOVEMBER				
S	M	T	W	T	F	S
					1	2
3	4	5	6	7	8	9
10	11	12	13	14	15	16
17	18	19	20	21	22	23
24	25	26	27	28	29	30

MONDAY 25

Moon in Scorpio.

TUESDAY 26

New Moon in Sagittarius; Venus enters Capricorn: An excellent day to get ahead with adventurous projects. Particular news may spur you on to take practical steps to follow your dreams.

WEDNESDAY 27

Venus square Chiron: if your plans are opposed, look for practical ways to get ahead and avoid taking random comments personally. Moon in Sagittarius.

THURSDAY 28

Mercury trine Neptune; Venus trine Uranus: it's a great day for art, music, meetings, romance and communications, although events will have a momentum of their own, so check you're on the right path and make adjustments accordingly. Moon enters Capricorn.

FRIDAY 29   )

Moon in Capricorn.

SATURDAY 30   )

Mercury sextile Saturn: A good day to make agreements and to take practical steps towards a goal. Moon enters Aquarius.

SUNDAY 1   )

Moon in Aquarius.

		NOVEMBER				
S	M	T	W	T	F	S
					1	2
3	4	5	6	7	8	9
10	11	12	13	14	15	16
17	18	19	20	21	22	23
24	25	26	27	28	29	30

MONDAY 2

Jupiter enters Capricorn: you may be inclined to focus on practicalities and realities in life rather than unrealistic expectations over the coming year. Moon in Aquarius.

TUESDAY 3

Mercury sextile Pluto; Venus sextile Mars: choose words carefully, and you could attain a goal. You may be enticed to indulge in delights. Romance could blossom. Moon enters Pisces.

WEDNESDAY 4

Moon in Pisces.

THURSDAY 5

Moon enters Aries.

FRIDAY 6

Moon in Aries.

SATURDAY 7

Moon in Aries.

SUNDAY 8

Sun square Neptune: Avoid romanticizing events, forgetfulness and excessive daydreaming. Your intuition may be on top form. Moon enters Taurus.

	DECEMBER					
S	M	T	W	T	F	S
1	2	3	4	5	6	7
8	9	10	11	12	13	14
15	16	17	18	19	20	21
22	23	24	25	26	27	28
29	30	31				

MONDAY 9 ●

Mercury enters Sagittarius; Jupiter square Chiron: you may feel more outgoing and more talkative over the coming weeks, and ready to help others.
Moon in Taurus.

TUESDAY 10 ●

Mercury semi-sextile Jupiter: a good day to talk and consider financial and travel plans. Moon enters Gemini.

WEDNESDAY 11 ●

Venus conjunct Saturn: a good day to consider making a commitment, for talks, meetings and considering financial matters. Moon in Gemini.

THURSDAY 12 ●

Full Moon in Gemini: a fresh phase will begin, especially regarding paperwork, writing, publishing, media, communications or travel. Ensure you are well -informed and be practical. Avoid impulsive decisions.

FRIDAY 13 ●

Venus conjunct Pluto; Mars trine Neptune: romance, money, and consideration of your values may arise. This is a transformative time. You may be idealistic, and matters may progress under their own steam, so ensure you're happy with the direction they take. Moon enters Cancer.

SATURDAY 14 ●

Mars sesquiquadrate Chiron: avoid impulsiveness. Moon in Cancer.

SUNDAY 15 ●

Jupiter trine Uranus: you may feel buoyant; a happy coincidence may occur; a surprise may arise. A promising day. Moon enters Leo.

DECEMBER

S	M	T	W	T	F	S
1	2	3	4	5	6	7
8	9	10	11	12	13	14
15	16	17	18	19	20	21
22	23	24	25	26	27	28
29	30	31				

MONDAY 16 ◗

Moon in Leo.

TUESDAY 17 ◗

Moon enters Virgo.

WEDNESDAY 18 ◗

Moon in Virgo.

THURSDAY 19 ◗

Mars sextile Saturn: a good day to take the initiative, especially at work.
Moon enters Libra.

FRIDAY 20   ☽

Mercury square Neptune: keep an eye on details; avoid forgetfulness. Look out for communication mix-ups and plan your travel route ahead to avoid delays. Moon in Libra.

SATURDAY 21   ☽

Moon enters Scorpio.

SUNDAY 22   ☽

Sun enters Capricorn; winter solstice: a time to assimilate accomplishments; a great day for a get-together. Venus square Uranus; Mars sextile Pluto: an unexpected event may occur; your emotions and passions may run high. You can make changes you would like to see but must avoid impulsiveness. Moon in Scorpio.

		DECEMBER				
S	M	T	W	T	F	S
1	2	3	4	5	6	7
8	9	10	11	12	13	14
15	16	17	18	19	20	21
22	23	24	25	26	27	28
29	30	31				

DECEMBER 2019

Sun enters Capricorn, December 22nd

As the Sun steps into Capricorn this marks the winter solstice in the northern hemisphere, a time when we collectively reflect on the hard work we have done all year and prepare for the New Year.

The Sun's alignment at this solstice with upbeat and jovial Jupiter and Uranus – (the planets astrologers associate with sudden or revolutionary change) – may contribute to the groundswell of change that is in the air, and for some – especially earth signs – this may be stabilizing and provide security.

But if developments create a sense of being stuck, there should be light at the end of the tunnel, as long as you can see that developments are in line with carefully laid plans.

However, if you find events simply gain a momentum of their own, take time out and reconsider your circumstances, carefully and in detail. A real pitfall would be to make impulsive decisions at this time, especially at the total solar eclipse on Boxing Day, December 26th. Avoid focussing on the negatives at this time, especially to do with family, property or your spiritual development. Focus instead on following your sense of purpose, your heart and your intuition, and you should discover the magic this time of the year will bring your way.

For more about the Sun in Capricorn in January 2020, see your 2020 Astrology Diary here: www.rockpoolpublishing.com.au

Wishing everyone a very happy solstice and Yuletide, and a Merry Christmas!

For Capricorns:

You tend to dislike abrupt, unexpected or simply uncalled-for change. And yet, you've learned how to work with change by managing it well.

The next four weeks will be par for the course, as you'll enjoy some developments, while others may simply be a thorn in the rose. Some developments may harken back to events in July. The key to your happiness now will be in how you react to developments – and how well you can assimilate change into your everyday life.

The period December 22nd to 31st will feature many developments that you'll love, and will make your heart sing. Those that don't, can be managed with your usual down-to-earth nature. A key to success? Being aware that the next ten days will gain their own momentum, and if you dislike the direction some developments are heading in, raise a flag earlier rather than later. Trust your instincts.

And, if you love the crackling good fun this time of year tends to bring, raise a toast to the joy and laughter and enjoy the seasonal spirit. Avoid intensifying domestic dynamics towards Christmas Day and the total solar eclipse on Boxing Day, especially if they skew towards what isn't working. Instead, focus on what is working in your family and life in general; and take it from there as you lead the way into a happy new year.

MONDAY 23   (

Moon enters Sagittarius.

TUESDAY 24   (

Sun trine Uranus; Mercury semi-sextile Pluto: a good day for get-togethers and to talk. A trip could lead to change. Moon in Sagittarius.

WEDNESDAY 25   (

Merry Christmas! Mercury semi-sextile Mars: you'll enjoy socializing and giving your ideas full rein. Avoid over-indulgence and speaking without forethought. Moon enters Capricorn.

THURSDAY 26   ○

Total (annular) solar eclipse in Capricorn: a good time to make plans, begin a new project and to strategize.

FRIDAY 27   )

Moon in Capricorn.

SATURDAY 28   )

Sun conjunct Jupiter: a trip, big idea or optimistic day will encourage you to relax or to consider a grand plan. Moon enters Aquarius.

SUNDAY 29   )

Mercury enters Capricorn: consider your plans in practical terms over the coming weeks. Moon in Aquarius.

| | | DECEMBER | | | | |
S	M	T	W	T	F	S
1	2	3	4	5	6	7
8	9	10	11	12	13	14
15	16	17	18	19	20	21
22	23	24	25	26	27	28
29	30	31				

MONDAY 30 ☽

Mercury square Chiron: avoid misunderstandings and traffic snarls; plan ahead for the best results. Moon enters Pisces.

TUESDAY 31 ☽

Happy New Year! Moon in Pisces.

WEDNESDAY 1

THURSDAY 2

FRIDAY 3

SATURDAY 4

SUNDAY 5

		DECEMBER				
S	M	T	W	T	F	S
1	2	3	4	5	6	7
8	9	10	11	12	13	14
15	16	17	18	19	20	21
22	23	24	25	26	27	28
29	30	31				

NOTES

NOTES

NOTES

NOTES

NOTES

NOTES

About the author

Patsy has worked as a professional astrologer for over 20 years. She began reading palms and tarot at age 14, and experienced mediumistic insights as young as 12. Patsy provides astrology and psychic intuitive readings and facilitates astrology and psychic development workshops in northern NSW.

Born in New Zealand, Patsy relocated to the UK where, in the 1980s, she worked as a sub-editor and production editor for women's and fashion magazines, including *Woman's Own* and *ELLE (UK)*.

She studied astrology at the Faculty of Astrological Studies in London in the 1990s and, in 1998, relocated to Australia, where she worked as a reporter for local newspapers in the Northern NSW area and continued to practise astrology.

Patsy has gained a Master of Arts degree in Romance Languages and Literature at the University of London. She is a member of the Queensland Federation of Astrologers and the Spiritualists National Union.

She has appeared on several live daytime TV and radio shows including *Studio 10* and *Mornings*, Channel 9, and her horoscopes are published in over 65 newspapers and magazines throughout Australia, including *The Sunshine Coast Daily*, *The West Australian* and *The Queensland Times*. Her monthly astrology blogs are published online in *Nature & Health* magazine and her articles have been published in many magazines including *Take 5* and *Practical Parenting*. Patsy's first astrology book, *Astrology: Secrets of the Moon* was published in October 2015 by Rockpool Publishing.

Patsy also runs www.astrocast.com.au; www.patsybennett.com and facebook/Astrocast1.

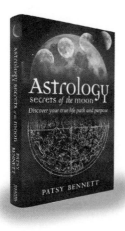

Available online at www.rockpoolpublishing.com.au or at all good book stores

FURTHER ASTRONOMICAL DATA:

The American Ephemeris for the 21st Century 2000 to 2050, Michelsen, ACS Publications.

COMPUTER PROGRAMS FOR ASTRONOMICAL DATA:

Solar Fire, Esoteric Technologies Pty Ltd

A note from the author

I hope you have enjoyed using this diary. You may like to have your own personalized astrological forecasts, as these are tailor-made to your birth data, and are precise for your individual needs. If you would like an analysis of your birth (natal) chart, you will need to know your time of birth as well as the place and date of your birth. Please feel free to contact me via email at: patsybennettastrology@gmail.com

Many thanks, Patsy

ORDER YOUR 2020 ASTROLOGY DIARY

Name...

Address...

City..State.........................

Postcode...........................Country...................................

Phone...

Email...

Mastercard ☐   Visa ☐

Credit card number..

Name on card...

Expiry date: ....CVV number........................

Please send me .... copies of

2020 Astrology Diary,

US$12.95 / GBP$8.99 per copy + US$3.95 / GBP$2.99 postage

To Place an Order in the USA
Red Wheel/Weiser/Conari
65 Parker Street, Suite 7
Newburyport, MA 01950, USA
Toll Free: 800.423.7087
orders@rwwbooks.com

To Place an Order in the UK
Deep Books Ltd
Goose Green Trading Estate,
47 E Dulwich Rd, East Dulwich,
London SE22 9BN, UK
sales@deep-books.co.uk
020 8693 0234 (UK)
+44 (0)20 8693 0234